Eyewitness
ANCIENT GREECE

Bronze mirror cover showing Aphrodite playing knucklebones with Pan, 350 BCE

Round - mouthed jug with coins

Griffin-head *oinochoe*

Bronze banqueter figurine

Aphrodite removing her sandal

Theseus and the minotaur

Kylix

Bronze chariot
ornament

Eyewitness
ANCIENT GREECE

Written by
ANNE PEARSON

DK Publishing

Wine strainer

Oil container

Bronze cymbals

DK

LONDON, NEW YORK,
MELBOURNE, MUNICH, and DELHI

Project editor Gillian Denton
Art editor Liz Sephton
Senior editor Helen Parker
Senior art editor Julia Harris
Production Louise Barratt
Picture research Diana Morris
Special photography Nick Nicolls
Additional photography Liz MacCaulay

THIS EDITION
Editor Sue Nicholson
Managing editor Camilla Hallinan
Managing art editor Martin Wilson
Publishing manager Sunita Gahir
Category publisher Andrea Pinnington
Art editor Catherine Goldsmith
Production editors Andy Hilliard, Laragh Kedwell, Hitesh Patel
Production controllers Angela Graef, Pip Tinsley
U.S. editors Margaret Parrish, John Searcy

This Eyewitness ® Guide has been conceived by
Dorling Kindersley Limited and Editions Gallimard

This edition first published in the United States in 2007
by DK Publishing, 375 Hudson Street, New York, NY 10014

Copyright © 1992, © 2004, © 2007, Dorling Kindersley Limited.

11 12 10 9 8 7
011 – AD336 – Jun/2007

A catalog record for this book is available
from the Library of Congress.

ISBN 978-0-7566-3002-7 (Hardcover)
978-0-7566-0648-0 (Library Binding)

Color reproduction by Colourscan, Singapore
Printed by Toppan Printing Co. (Shenzhen) Ltd., China

Terra-cotta
dancing woman

Terra-cotta
figurine of a
youth with hat

Griffin earrings

Rattle shaped like a pig

Discover more at
www.dk.com

Contents

Child's toy

6
The Greek world

8
Minoan civilization

10
The Mycenaean civilization

12
To Troy and back

14
Greek expansion

16
Athens, city of Athena

18
Power and politics in Athens

20
Gods, goddesses, and heroes

24
Festivals and oracles

26
Temples

28
At home

30
Women's world

32
Growing up in Greece

34
Fun and games

36
Wining and dining

38
A day out

40
Body beautiful

42
Clothes for comfort

44
The Greek games

46
Wisdom and beauty

48
Vases and vessels

50
Farming, fishing, and food

52
Crafts, travel, and trade

54
Warfare

56
The state of Sparta

58
Science and medicine

60
Death and the afterlife

62
Alexander and the Hellenistic age

64
Did you know?

66
Who's who

68
Find out more

70
Glossary

72
Index

The Greek world

THE LAND OF GREECE is made up of mainland Greece and the numerous islands scattered throughout the Aegean and Adriatic seas. It is a mountainous country with hot dry summers and rain only in winter. Early Greek settlements developed when small independent communities were cut off from each other by the mountains and were often competing for the best land, because fertile arable land is in short supply. Each of the city-states that developed out of these communities had a strong individual identity, and citizens were very loyal to their home state and to its patron deity. This miscellaneous collection of city-states sometimes joined together for mutual defense and did so most successfully against the Persians. The Greeks produced a glorious culture which has had a profound effect on western civilization, through succeeding centuries to the present day. They scaled the heights in literature, the visual and dramatic arts, in philosophy and politics, in sport, and in many other aspects of human life. Greek civilization reached its peak in Athens in the fifth century BCE.

THE BRITISH MUSEUM
The British Museum in London was inspired by classical Greek architecture. The first part of the building was completed in 1827 and the building as it is today gradually arose over the next 30 years. Many of the objects in this book can be seen there.

KOUROS
Kouroi (marble statues of naked boys), were made mainly in the sixth century BCE to decorate sanctuaries of the gods, especially Apollo, but some may have been put up in memory of young soldiers who had died in battle. They stand with their arms by their sides and one foot in front of the other.

THE ANCIENT GREEK WORLD
This map shows ancient Greece and the surrounding area. It includes towns established by the first emigrants from the mainland who traveled east. The emigrants settled on the coastal area of Asia Minor called Ionia. The names of the regions are in capitals and the cities are in small letters.

ACROPOLIS
The city of Athens (pp. 16–17) was the most important city of ancient Greece, and the main center for all forms of arts and learning. Its Acropolis was crowned with the temple of the Parthenon, dedicated to the goddess Athena.

DONKEY DRINKING CUP
Beautifully painted pottery was a specialty of the Greeks. It was used mainly for storing, mixing, serving, and drinking wine. This is a special two-handled cup in the form of a donkey's head.

HIPPOCAMP
This gold ring is decorated with a hippocamp, a seahorse with two forefeet and a body ending in the tail of a dolphin or a fish.

GREECE AND THE WIDER WORLD
This chart shows the rise and fall of the Greek world from Minoan times to the end of the Hellenistic period. These historic events can be seen against a background of other civilizations in Europe, Asia, and South America.

DATES BCE	2000–1500	1500–1100	1100–800	800–479	479–323	323–30
EVENTS IN GREECE	Cretan palace civilization	Fall of Knossos Rise and fall of Mycenean civilization	Earliest Greek cities in Iona	First Olympic Games Greek colonies in Black Sea and Sicily Persian invasions	Sparta controls Peloponnese Age of Perikles Rise of Macedon Life of Alexander	Wars of Alexander's successors Roman conquest
CULTURAL PERIOD	Bronze Age	Bronze Age	Early Iron Age	Archaic	Classical	Hellenistic
WORLD EVENTS	Indus Valley civilization in India Middle Kingdom in Egypt	Egyptian New Kingdom Hittite Empire Shang dynasty in China	Olmec civilization in Mexico Earliest Phoenician colonies	Rise of Etruscans in Italy Rome founded Assyrian Empire	Confucius born in China Buddha born in India Persian Empire	Qin and Han dynasties in China Mayan civilization in Central America

MARATHON MEN
Athletics was a favorite pastime in ancient Greece (pp. 44–45). Games took place as part of religious festivals. These three runners are painted on a pot which was given as a prize to the winner of the race at the Panathenaic Games held in Athens in honor of Athena (pp. 16–17).

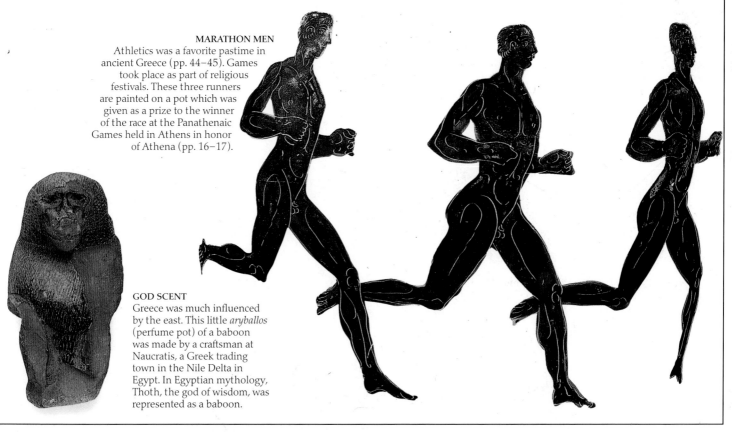

GOD SCENT
Greece was much influenced by the east. This little *aryballos* (perfume pot) of a baboon was made by a craftsman at Naucratis, a Greek trading town in the Nile Delta in Egypt. In Egyptian mythology, Thoth, the god of wisdom, was represented as a baboon.

Minoan civilization

DECORATING WITH DOLPHINS
The walls of the Minoan palaces were richly decorated with painted scenes known as frescoes, made by applying paint to wet plaster. Many we see today are modern reconstructions, based on fragments of painted plaster which have survived. This famous dolphin fresco is from the Queen's apartment at Knossos.

CRETE
This map shows the main towns and palaces on the island, at Knossos, Zakro, Phaestus, and Mallia. A large villa has also been found at Hagia Triada. Most of the settlements were built close to the sea. The remains of the lavish buildings are evidence of the skill of Minoan architects, engineers, and artists. Not everyone lived in the palaces. Some lived in smaller townhouses or in farmhouses in the country. It is said that the young Zeus was brought up in the Dictaean Cave on the high plain of Lassithi.

THE FIRST GREAT CIVILIZATION of the Aegean world flourished on the island of Crete. The early inhabitants settled as early as 6000 BCE, but the island reached the height of its power between 2200 BCE and 1450 BCE. Its wealth was due to its thriving trade with other Bronze Age towns in Greece, the Mediterranean, and in Egypt and Syria. Prosperity also came from the rich Cretan soil which produced oil, grain, and wine in abundance. The economy was based around rich palaces, the remains of which have been found in different parts of the island. This impressive Cretan civilization is known as Minoan after a legendary king of Crete called Minos. Knossos and the other palaces were all destroyed by fire around 1700 BCE, but after that they were rebuilt even more luxuriously. From then until about 1500 BCE, Minoan civilization was at its height.

WORSHIPER
This bronze figure is in an attitude of worship of the gods.

TAKING THE BULL BY THE HORNS
The bull was regarded by the Minoans as a sacred animal. A Greek myth tells the story of the god Zeus falling in love with a beautiful princess called Europa. Zeus turned himself into a white bull and swam to Crete with her on his back. They had three sons, one of whom was Minos, who became the king of Crete. Daring bull sports became a way of worshiping the bull. This bronze figure shows a boy somersaulting over the bull's horns.

BULL MURAL
This mural at Knossos also shows an acrobat leaping the bull.

DISCOVERING KNOSSOS
English archeologist Sir Arthur Evans (1851–1941) discovered the most famous of the Minoan palaces at Knossos in 1894. He dug there for several years, and the remains of the colossal building he found, with its hundreds of rooms, amazed the world.

THESEUS AND THE MINOTAUR
According to Greek legend, a young prince of Athens called Theseus went to Crete and killed a monster, half-man and half-bull, to whom Athenian children were sent as sacrifice each year. The monster, called the Minotaur, was kept in a maze called the Labyrinth. It is possible that the huge palace at Knossos may have resembled a Labyrinth because of its many long and winding corridors.

MODERN MINOTAUR
The story of the conflict between Theseus and the Minotaur was popular not only with Greek vase painters but also with many modern artists. This interpretation by Spanish artist Pablo Picasso (1881–1973) is almost as difficult to unravel as the maze!

RESTORATION AND RECONSTRUCTION
The palace of Knossos was built and rebuilt several times. It was made of stone with wooden roofs and ceilings. Some parts of it were four stories high. It had royal apartments, including a throne room where the ruler of Knossos would sit in splendor. Sir Arthur Evans restored some of the palace, so it is now possible to get a sense of what it was like when it was new. The wooden columns are painted the same shade of red as the original.

The Mycenaean civilization

Greece in the bronze age (before iron tools and weapons came into use), had several important centers, including Mycenae. Mycenae, city of the king Agamemnon, was one of several heavily fortified strongholds. The king, or chief, lived in a palace with many rooms which served as a military headquarters and a center of administration for the surrounding countryside. The Mycenaeans were warriors, and weapons and armor have been found in their graves. They were also great traders and sailed far and wide. Their civilization reached the height of its power in about 1600 BCE and eclipsed the Minoan civilization of Crete. All seemed secure and prosperous, but around 1250 BCE the Mycenaeans started to build huge defensive walls around all the major towns. The Mycenaean world was under threat from foreign invaders. By about 1200 BCE the cities began to be abandoned or destroyed. Within 100 years the Mycenaean strongholds had fallen and a period often called the Dark Ages had begun.

POMEGRANATE PENDANT
This little gold pendant in the form of a pomegranate was found in Cyprus. It was made by a Mycenaean craftsman around 1300 BCE and is a good example of a jewelry technique called granulation. Tiny gold granules grouped in triangles decorate the surface of the pomegranate. Mycenaean artists and traders settled in Cyprus in large numbers. The island later provided a refuge for many Greeks fleeing from unrest at home, as Mycenaean civilization crumbled.

OCTOPUS JAR
This pottery jar with a painting of an octopus was found in a cemetery at a Mycenaean colony on the island of Rhodes. Mycenaean artists were very influenced by Minoan work and subjects like this, inspired by the sea, continued to be popular.

BULL SPRINKLER
This clay bull's head was used as a ritual sprinkler at religious ceremonies. There are small holes in the mouth to let the water escape. Although these sprinklers are sometimes in the shape of other animals, bulls are the most common.

GRAVE CIRCLE

In 1876, a royal burial ground at Mycenae was excavated by Heinrich Schliemann (pp.12-13). It consisted of a number of shaft graves enclosed by a low circular wall. A great deal of gold jewelry, which can be dated to around 1600 B.C., was found in these graves. Its discovery confirmed the words of Homer, who described Mycenae as "rich in gold."

THE TREASURY OF ATREUS

The treasury of Atreus at Mycenae was the finest of the great beehive shaped tombs built there from c. 1500 BC. The shape over the entrance is identical to that of the lion gate shown left.

LION GATE

Mycenae, most powerful of the Mycenaean cities, gave its name to the civilization. It lies on a low hill in the Peloponnesus, the peninsula forming the southern part of Greece. The city walls, built about 1250 B.C., were made of huge blocks of stone. The main entrance to the citadel was a gateway in the walls, now called the Lion Gate. Wide enough for carts, it was decorated with sculptures of two lions on either side of a pillar, perhaps the symbol of the Mycenaean royal family.

CUTTLEFISH CUP

Mycenaean potters and other artists often worked for the king and had their workshops close to the palace. The shape of this graceful drinking cup, with its long stem, was invented by the Mycenaeans. It is decorated with stylized cuttlefish.

MASK OF AGAMEMNON

Five of the royal persons buried in the shaft graves of Mycenae wore funeral masks of beaten gold. When Schliemann removed one of the masks, for a moment he could see the dried face of the corpse beneath. The mask shown here was thought by Schliemann to belong to Agamemnon, the legendary king of Mycenae at the time of the Trojan War (pp. 12-13). Schliemann was wrong – the mask seems to have belonged to an earlier time – but the name persists.

BIRD WOMEN

Thousands of little terra-cotta figures in the form of women have been found at Mycenaean sites. They have beak-like noses and prominent breasts and may represent a fertility goddess. They wear flat headdresses and long skirts and hold up their arms in an attitude of worship.

To Troy and back

IN THE 12TH CENTURY BCE, the rich Mycenaean towns and palaces fell into a decline or were destroyed, trade with the east decreased, and Greece entered a dark age. During the next few centuries, stories of the great Mycenaean civilization that had gone before were handed down from one generation to the next in the form of poems. Two of them, *The Iliad* and *The Odyssey*, have survived. They reached their final form in the eighth century BCE in the hands of the poet Homer, whose poetry was admired throughout the Greek world. *The Iliad* describes how a city called Troy, on the west coast of modern Turkey, was besieged by a Greek army led by King Agamemnon of Mycenae. It describes the heroic deeds of Greek and Trojan soldiers like Achilles and Hektor. *The Odyssey* tells the story of the return home from the Trojan War of one Greek hero, Odysseus. It took him ten years and he had many dangerous adventures. The Homeric stories reflect real incidents of wars, battles, and sieges from an earlier age. It is probable that war was waged between the Greeks and the Trojans, possibly over the ownership of lands and crops at a time when the Mycenaean world was falling apart, and not over the recapture of Helen (above).

HEINRICH SCHLIEMANN
In 1870, German archeologist Heinrich Schliemann (1822–1890), discovered the site of ancient Troy near the Mediterranean coast in modern Turkey. He had been looking for it for many years. His excavations revealed not just one city, but more than nine of them, built on top of each other. (It is not certain which layer is the city described in *The Iliad*). Schliemann's wife is wearing some of the superb jewelry found at Troy.

HELEN OF TROY
Helen was the beautiful wife of Menelaus, king of Sparta and brother of Agamemnon, king of Mycenae. According to legend, Helen's capture by Paris, son of Priam, king of Troy, was the cause of the Trojan War. The Greeks united to defeat the Trojans and restore Helen to her husband.

OVERCOME BY CURIOSITY
Troy withstood the Greeks' siege for ten long years. In the end, the Greeks triumphed by a trick. They constructed a huge wooden horse which they left just outside the city. The Trojans then watched the Greek army sail away, and overcome with curiosity, dragged the horse inside the city walls. Late that night, Greek soldiers, hidden inside the horse, crept out and opened the city gates. The Greek army, which had silently returned, entered and destroyed the city. This picture of the horse comes from a pot of about 650–600 BCE.

MODERN MODEL
In Troy today, there is a modern replica of the Trojan horse. It is very large and, like the ancient one, is made of wood. Children can climb a ladder into its stomach and pretend to be Greek soldiers.

THE WOODEN HORSE
The story of Troy and the wooden horse has been a favorite with artists through the centuries. Italian artist Giovanni Tiepolo (1696–1770), painted more than one version of the subject.

THE BLINDING OF POLYPHEMUS

In one of his adventures on his way home from the Trojan war, the hero Odysseus met a Cyclops called Polyphemus, a man-eating giant with only one eye in the middle of his forehead. Odysseus and his men were trapped in Polyphemus' cave and the giant started to eat them one by one. Cunning Odysseus brought the giant a skin full of wine, which lulled him into a drunken sleep. Then he blinded Polyphemus by driving a red-hot stake into his only eye.

PATIENT PENELOPE

After his ten-year journey, Odysseus returned at last to Ithaca, his island home, and to his wife Penelope. During his long absence, she had waited patiently for him, even though everyone else had given him up for dead. When other men proposed marriage to Penelope, she told them that she would give them an answer when she had finished weaving a particular piece of cloth. At night, Penelope crept secretly to her loom, and undid everything she had woven during the day. In this way, she postponed indefinitely her reply to her suitors. In this painting by British artist John Stanhope (1829–1908), Penelope is sitting sadly beside her loom.

WOOLLY ESCAPE

Polyphemus kept a flock of sheep in the cave at night and these provided a means of escape. Odysseus and his men tied themselves underneath the sheep. In the morning, the flock filed out of the cave to graze. The blind giant felt the backs of the sheep in case his captives were hiding there, but he did not think of feeling under their bellies. This story has been illustrated on a black-figured vase.

Blue paint indicating sea

Helmet

MOTHER TO THE RESCUE

The mother of Achilles was a sea nymph called Thetis. This little terra-cotta figurine shows Thetis, or one of her sisters, riding the waves on a seahorse, bringing a new helmet for Achilles to wear in battle. Some of the bright blue paint, representing the sea, still survives.

DEATH OF A HERO

After the Greek champion, Achilles, had killed the bravest Trojan warrior, Hektor, he tied his body to a chariot and dragged it three times around the walls of Troy. On this clay lamp, Achilles can be seen driving the chariot and looking back in triumph. Above him, on the walls of Troy, Hektor's parents, King Priam and Queen Hecuba, watch in horror.

Greek expansion

GREECE STARTED TO EMERGE from the Dark Ages in the eighth century BCE. Trading posts began to be established abroad, even as far away as the Nile Delta in Egypt. As the population expanded and Greek agriculture proved insufficient to meet the needs of the people, some towns sent out colonies both east- and westward. They settled in southern Italy, Sicily, and other parts of the western Mediterranean, and in the East around the shores of the Black Sea. Some of these colonies were very rich. It was said that the people of Sybaris in southern Italy slept on beds of rose petals, and roosters were banned from the town so that the inhabitants would not be woken too early in the morning. Greek culture was influenced by foreign styles. The Geometric style, which, as its name suggests, was dominated by geometric patterns, gave way to a new, so-called Orientalizing style. Designs influenced by the East, such as griffins and sphinxes, were introduced. Egypt and Syria were the main sources. Corinth, Rhodes, and Ephesus were well placed for eastern trade and became rich.

GOLDEN GRIFFINS
These gold griffin heads, inspired by the East, were found on the island of Rhodes. They were made in the seventh century BCE and were once attached to a pair of earrings.

MAN SIZE
The Greeks liked to wear bangles decorated with animal heads. This lion-headed bangle, which is silver-plated, may have been worn by a man.

FOND FAREWELL
This detail is from a large pot decorated in the Geometric style. The figures are rigid and painted in silhouette. The man on the right is stepping onto a boat and leaving the woman. Perhaps he is meant to be the hero Odysseus saying goodbye to his wife Penelope before he goes off to the Trojan War (pp. 12–13), or possibly he is Paris abducting Helen.

FAIENCE FROG
At this time in Greek history, there was much interest in Egyptian art and the craftsman who made this may have been copying Egyptian work. It shows a man kneeling and holding a jar on top of which is a frog, a sacred creature in Egyptian religion. The object is made of faience, a greenish material often used to make Egyptian ornaments.

LION *ARYBALLOS*
This *aryballos* (perfume pot), which probably came from Thebes, has a spout in the shape of a lion's head. In spite of its small size, it has three zones of painted figures upon it. Warriors can be seen walking in procession, and there is also a horse race. At the bottom is a tiny scene of dogs chasing hares. The mouth of this pot would have been filled with wax to prevent the evaporation of the perfume inside.

EXOTIC EXPORTS
Many little perfume pots were made in the town of Corinth and exported all over the Greek world. They are often in curious shapes and prettily decorated. The winged figure painted on this one may represent a god of the wind.

GREEK COLONIZATION

The new colonies were established in places with good harbors and agricultural land. The process of colonization started as early as 750 BCE and continued to about 550 BCE. These new colonies soon became independent of their mother cities in Greece.

PRICKLY PERFUME

This *aryballos*, in the form of a hedgehog, was found in a Greek trading colony at Naucratis in the Nile Delta.

GROOMING

These four Geometric style clay horses form the handle of a lid of a *pyxis*, a pot in which women kept their cosmetics and combs. Compared with the perfectly formed horses of later Greek art they may seem a bit crude, but they have a liveliness about them that can also be seen in the bronze work of this period.

Athens, city of Athena

THE ACROPOLIS
In early times, the Acropolis (high city) of Athens was a fortified citadel. Later, it became the most sacred part of the town where many important temples and sanctuaries were situated.

ATHENS WAS THE MOST POWERFUL of all the Greek city-states. It was also a great center of the arts and learning. Its patron, Athena, was goddess of wisdom and warfare, and perfectly symbolized the two sides of her city's life. In 480 BCE, Athens was attacked by the Persians and the temples on the Acropolis were destroyed. Later, when Athens had played a leading role in the Persian wars (pp. 54–55) and successfully defended Greece, a huge rebuilding program was launched by the leader of Athens, Perikles (pp. 18–19). Athens was situated in an area called Attica and was more densely populated than other Greek cities. The people of Athens lived on the land below the Acropolis. Many fine public squares and colonnaded buildings have been found there around the *agora*, an open space for meeting and commercial activity. Nearby was the port of Athens, the Piraeus. Access to the sea was a main reason for Athens' miltary and economic successes.

SACRED STATUE
The purpose of the procession shown on the frieze (sculptured panel) was to bring a new dress for a sacred wooden statue of Athena at the Acropolis. The dress, a woven *peplos* (pp. 42–43), is being handed to a

THE ERECHTHEION
The Erechtheion, called after a legendary king of Athens, was a smaller temple than the Parthenon. It probably housed the wooden statue of Athena. Its famous porch has marble statues of women (*caryatids*) instead of columns, holding up the roof.

THE PARTHENON FRIEZE
The marble frieze of the Parthenon went around all four sides of the temple and was set up high, on the outside of the central chambers near the ceiling of the colonnade.

Its main subject was the procession of worshipers which wound its way up from the *agora* to the Acropolis every four years as a part of the festival called the Great Panathenaea in honor of the goddess Athena. Young men on horseback take up much of the frieze.

THE PARTHENON
The temple of the Parthenon occupies the highest point of the Acropolis. It was dedicated to Athena. The word Parthenon comes from the Greek word *parthenos* meaning virgin. Athena was sometimes described as Athena Parthenos. The Parthenon, which still stands today, was built between 447 and 432 BCE. The sculptures which decorated it were designed by Pheidias.

GOLDEN GODDESS
Inside the Parthenon stood a huge gold and ivory statue of the goddess Athena, made by the famous sculptor Pheidias, a close friend of Perikles. She appears in all her splendor as goddess of warfare. In this replica, based on a smaller copy of the original statue and on descriptions by Greek writers, she wears her *aegis*, a small goatskin cloak fringed with snakes, and a high-crested helmet. On her right hand is a small winged figure of Nike, the goddess of victory.

An Athenian coin showing an owl, the bird of Athena

THE ELGIN MARBLES
Many of the sculptures from the Parthenon were brought to England by Lord Elgin, the British ambassador to the Ottoman court. He saw the sculptures when he visited Athens and was granted permission to bring some back to England. They can be seen today in the British Museum.

Temporary Elgin Room at the British Museum painted by A. Archer

Some young men are trotting gently along and others are galloping with their cloaks flying out behind them. The background to the frieze was originally painted, probably a bright blue. The horses used to have bridles of bronze.

The bridles have not survived, leaving only traces of the holes where they were attached to the marble. In the south frieze, a number of young cows can be seen. In other parts of the frieze, women are carrying sacrificial vessels, bowls, and jugs.

Power and politics in Athens

ANCIENT GREECE WAS MADE UP of a number of independent city-states. There were very few rich people and a great number of poor. In early times, the rich landowners and leaders called tyrants controlled the poor. In Athens and some other city-states the tyrants were driven out by the people, who acquired power and freedom. This new form of government was called democracy. It was invented in Athens. The Assembly was the main forum of political life. Meetings took place on a hill called the Pnyx near the Acropolis. Ordinary citizens, rich or poor, could make a speech and vote at the Assembly. At least 6,000 people had to be present for a meeting to take place. The Assembly made important decisions, for example, whether or not to declare war. A higher government body was a Council of 500 members, which arranged the business for the Assembly. It met in a round building called the *tholos*. In times of war, decisions were made about the defense of the city by a group of ten military commanders called *strategoi*. These were elected annually and could be reelected many times.

PERIKLES

Perikles was an Athenian statesman and general. A powerful orator, he was elected *strategos* every year from 443 to 429 BCE. Athens prospered under his rule, and he was responsible for the rebuilding of the Acropolis after its destruction during the Persian wars (490s and '80s BCE.). On this Roman copy of a Greek bust of Perikles, his name has been inscribed in Greek.

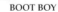

BOOT BOY

This little bronze figure is of an African boy holding a shoe. Athenian society depended on slaves. Some were prisoners of war and some foreigners bought from slave traders. Most of the housework in wealthy Athenian homes was done by slaves. Other heavy work, such as working in the silver mines in southern Attica, was also done by slaves. A few slaves might receive wages from their masters and be able to buy back their freedom. Others, such as the tutors employed to teach the sons of rich families, may have been treated with respect, but most slaves probably led lives of drudgery.

PALACE OF WESTMINSTER

Many modern governments have been strongly influenced by the democratic system which developed in Athens in the fifth century BCE. The word democracy is Greek and it means "power of the people." It was not, however, a democracy as the term is used today, because a large chunk of Greek society, including women, foreigners, and slaves, did not have the vote.

TREASURY OF TRIUMPH

The battle of Marathon was a famous victory by the Greeks over the Persians in 490 BCE. Soon afterward this fine marble building was erected at Delphi by the Athenians as a symbol of triumph. It was a Treasury, full of Persian spoils, an expression of the prestige of Athens, and also a religious offering to Apollo at his holiest sanctuary. It stands in a prominent position beside the Sacred Way which winds up to the temple. This Treasury is a vivid illustration of the close links which existed between religion and politics in the ancient Greek world.

EXILE OF THEMISTOKLES

This coin shows an Athenian leader, Themistokles, whose main achievement was the creation of the fleet that enabled the Greeks to destroy the Persians at the battle of Salamis in 480 BCE (pp. 54–55). Later, he was ostracized (banished) from Athens. When citizens wished to banish a politician, they would write his name on a piece of pot, an *ostrakon*, and these were counted. If more than 6,000 votes were cast he had to leave Athens for ten years.

It is rare to find Greek inscriptions on bronze: usually they were carved in stone

JUDGMENT TABLET

This oblong tablet contains a treaty between the cities of Oiantheia and Chaleion. The two sides agreed that there should be a legal process for solving disputes about the ownership of land, with penalties if the treaty was broken by either side.

The carved figures at the top represent Democracy crowning the Athenian People

The decree is carved with the letters in a grid pattern, with no spaces between words—a style called stoichedon

ANTITYRANNY LAW

The inscription on this *stele* (upright stone slab) outlines the Athenian law against tyranny, which was introduced by Eucrates in 336 BCE. Eucrates' law was just one of several decrees passed by the Assembly which were designed to protect the democratic govenment of Athens.

Gods, goddesses, and heroes

DIONYSOS FROM DELOS
Dionysos was the god of wine and earth fertility. In this mosaic from the island of Delos, he is riding a leopard.

THE GREEKS BELIEVED that all the gods were descendants of Gaia (the earth) and Uranos (the sky). They thought the gods were probably much like humans: they fell in love with each other, married, quarreled, had children, played music, and in many other ways mirrored human characteristics (or humans mirrored theirs). All the gods had their own spheres of influence. Demeter and Persephone were responsible for the grain growing, Artemis was the goddess of hunting, Apollo could foretell the future, and Aphrodite was the goddess of love. Many of the best-known gods had temples and sanctuaries dedicated to them, and much money and artistic ability were lavished on these places. Religion played a large part in the lives of ordinary people. Indeed, most of the beautiful buildings that still survive are temples. Worshipers believed that the gods would treat them well and meet their needs if they offered them animal sacrifices and the fruits of the harvest.

THE KING OF THE GODS
Zeus was the king of the gods. He usually appears in art as a strong, middle-aged, bearded man of great power and dignity. Sometimes he carries his symbol, a thunderbolt.

HOME OF THE GODS
Mount Olympus is the highest mountain in Greece and was believed to be the home of the gods. It is in the north of Greece, on the borders of Thessaly and Macedonia.

GODDESS OF LOVE
This bronze head of Aphrodite comes from eastern Turkey. The goddess was born from the sea foam and believed to have been carried by the Zephyrs (West Winds) to Cyprus. Although she was married to Hephaistos, she fell in love with Ares, the god of war.

BEAUTY AND THE BEAST
On this mirror case, the goddess Aphrodite is playing a game of knucklebones (pp. 34–35) with the god Pan. The goddess of love and beauty is often shown by artists as a graceful young woman, with the upper part of her body bare. She is accompanied by Eros (according to some myths, her son), shown here as a small, winged boy, and a goose, a symbol associated with her. Pan was a god of the countryside and had goat's legs and ears.

20

BRAIN CHILD
The strange birth of Athena was a favorite subject for Greek vase painters. She was the daughter of Zeus by the goddess Metis, meaning wisdom. Zeus was told that any son born to Metis would be more powerful than its father, and so, hoping to prevent this, he swallowed Metis. Soon afterward, Zeus was seized by fierce pains in his head. He ordered the god Hephaistos to cut it open, and Athena emerged.

Apollo and Daphne by Italian artist Antonio del Pollaiuolo (1432–1498)

APOLLO AND DAPHNE
Daphne was a nymph loved by Apollo. According to one myth he tried to seize her, but she escaped. In answer to her prayer, Zeus turned her into a laurel tree, ironically, the tree sacred to Apollo.

HEPHAISTOS
The lame god Hephaistos, who was a smith, made a special ax to cut open Zeus' head. He also made a throne and shield for the king of the gods. He was the god of fire and husband of Aphrodite.

APOLLO
Apollo, a beautiful young deity, was the twin brother of Artemis, the goddess of the hunt. He had a famous shrine and oracle at Delphi. He is associated with the Sun, with light, and with healing and medicine.

ATHENA
Athena was the patron goddess of the city of Athens. She was also the goddess of wisdom and warfare, and presided over the arts, literature, and philosophy. Her favorite bird was the owl and her favorite plant the olive tree, which she is credited with introducing to Athens. In the Trojan war (pp. 12–13) she fought on the side of the Greeks, and assisted Odysseus in his long voyage home.

DEMETER AND PERSEPHONE
Demeter and Persephone were mother and daughter and goddesses of the grain. This terra-cotta figure shows them sitting side by side wearing headdresses. They were probably holding the reins of an oxcart, which has not survived the years.

Continued on next page **21**

THE FAUN
In this painting by the Italian artist Piero di Cosimo (1462–1521), a woman lies dead, mourned by a faun and a dog. Fauns were identified with the god Pan, who was the protector of shepherds and their flocks.

EROS AND PSYCHE
Greek myths were a mixture of stories about gods and heroes. The stories grew with the telling, and there were many different versions. Gods and heroes gained or lost popularity at different periods of Greek history. This Hellenistic terracotta shows Eros, the god who makes people fall in love, kissing Psyche, the goddess who represents the soul. To the ancient Greeks, their embrace symbolized perfect happiness.

HERAKLES
The greatest hero of all, Herakles, was the son of Zeus by a mortal woman. As a tiny baby Herakles proved he was a hero by strangling with his bare hands two snakes sent to attack him. In adult life, Herakles performed twelve famous Labors (tasks) for a king called Eurystheus. In the first Labor, Herakles killed the Nemean lion, and is often shown, as on this vase, wearing its skin. The Labor shown here is the killing of the Stymphalian birds. These birds, which lived near a lake in the northeast Peloponnese, destroyed crops and wounded people with their poisonous feathers. Herakles scared them with a bronze rattle, given to him by the smith god Hephaistos (pp. 20–21), and then shot them with a sling. Herakles was strong and courageous, but he liked wine and women and had many love affairs.

THE BUILDING OF THE ARGO

This Roman terra-cotta wall panel shows a scene from the famous myth of Jason and the Argonauts. Jason was a prince from Thessaly in northern Greece, and the Argonauts were a group of heroes who sailed with him on a ship they had built called the *Argo*. Heroes often battled with strange monsters, and often undertook long and difficult journeys. Jason and his crew set sail to find the Golden Fleece which hung on a tree near the Black Sea, and was guarded by a snake. The goddess Athena helped Jason in this task and she can be seen on the left helping the crew to construct the *Argo*.

PEGASUS

This coin shows the winged horse Pegasus. Pegasus was tamed by the hero Bellerophon, who tried to ride him to heaven. But Pegasus was stung by a gadfly sent by Zeus and threw Bellerophon off his back and down to Earth.

TOO HIGH!

Icarus was the son of Daedalus, a mythical craftsman who made wings for himself and his son, to enable them to fly. Their wings were attached by wax. Icarus flew too high, the heat of the Sun melted the wax, and he fell into the Aegean Sea and drowned.

LURE OF THE LYRE

Orpheus was a poet and a musician. He played the lyre and the kithara and sang so well that he could tame wild animals; trees and plants would bend their branches to him, and he could soothe the most violent of tempers. He took part in the expedition of Jason and the Argonauts and calmed the crew and stilled the waves with his music. In this beautiful painting by Dutch painter Roelandt Savery (1576–1639), the magic of Orpheus' music is illustrated. All the birds and beasts are lying down together in an enchanted landscape.

PERSEUS AND MEDUSA

On this vase painting of 460 BCE, the hero Perseus has just cut off the head of the gorgon Medusa. One look from Medusa could turn a person to stone, which is why Perseus beheaded her. Her head can be seen in Perseus' bag.

Festivals and oracles

COME DANCING
A row of people join hands and approach an altar where a sacrifice is blazing, at a festival in the countryside. A priestess, or perhaps Demeter, the corn goddess, stands behind the altar with a flat basket used for winnowing grain.

RELIGION PLAYED A MAJOR PART in Greek life. Greek worship centered around a small altar at home, usually in the courtyard of the house. The Greeks believed that they could strike a bargain with the gods. They offered them gold, silver, and animal sacrifice. They also held festivals and games in their honor. In return, they expected the gods to protect them from illness, look after their crops, and grant other favors. Communication with the gods had a regular place in the calendar; most festivals took place once a year, or sometimes every four years. Gods were also worshiped in sanctuaries—one of the most important was that of Apollo at Delphi. Apollo was well-known as a god of prophecy, and at Delphi he would reply to questions about the future. His priestess would act as the mouthpiece of the god and make obscure pronouncements which could be interpreted in different ways. The oracle (as these forecasts were called) at Delphi lasted into Christian times.

HOLY BULL
A bull was one of the animals offered at important sacrificial occasions. Bulls were decorated with garlands of plants and ribbons to show that they had been set aside for the gods. Garlanded bulls' heads were the inspiration for some of the decorative patterns on temples.

SOMETHING OLD, SOMETHING NEW
The huge columns of a Greek temple at ancient Poseidonia (Paestum) in southern Italy frame a bride and groom posing for their wedding photos. Ancient ruins like these are believed to bring good luck to a new marriage.

CENTER OF THE WORLD
Delphi was thought to be the center of the world, at the very point where two birds flying from opposite ends of the earth met. The Greeks placed a huge stone there, the *omphalos*, or navel of the world. A network of woolen strands—a sign that this was a holy object— is carved on this version, which is in the museum at Delphi.

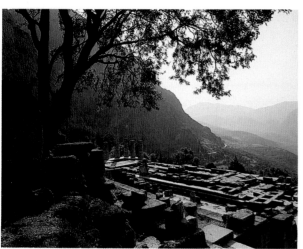

THE CHARIOTEER

A stadium was built high above the temple to Apollo at Delphi, for games and chariot races in honor of the god. Winning the chariot race was the greatest honor of the games, and the owner of the winning team of horses paid for a statue to celebrate his success. The eyes of this magnificent bronze statue are inlaid with glass and stone, the lips are copper, and the headband is patterned with silver. The charioteer is still holding the reins of his horses even though they have long disappeared. This is one of the best-known statues of ancient Greece.

TEMPLE OF APOLLO

Delphi was the home of the main shrine of Apollo. It lies on the steep slopes of Mount Parnassus, the favorite haunt of Apollo and also of the Muses, who looked after arts and music. A road lined with small buildings, to house the rich gifts made to the god, still winds its way up the slope and past the remains of his great temple, which housed the oracle.

SANCTUARY OF ATHENA

The sanctuary of Athena lies farther down the mountain from Apollo's shrine. In the middle of it is this circular building, the purpose of which is unknown. It is set against the silvery blue background of thousands of olive trees. Athena was supposed to have created the olive tree, and these groves still provide a rich harvest for local people.

THE WAY TO ATHENA

In the goddess Athena's own city of Athens lay the Panathenaic Way, a special road that led up to her temples and altars on the Acropolis. Leading up from the *agora*, the market and meeting place of the city, the road today passes the rebuilt version of a *stoa*, a long, colonnaded building. It was used for commerce and conversation.

PROCESSION OF SACRIFICE

On this broad bowl used for wine (the ivy leaves which decorate it are linked with Dionysus, the wine god), a long line of people are on their way to worship the goddess Athena. The altar where the flames are already rising is on the right of the bowl. Athena is standing behind the altar. The procession is led by a woman carrying a tray of cakes on her head. She is followed by a man leading the sacrificial bull, then a man playing the double pipes. The rest of the men in the procession carry all the objects necessary for the worship of the goddess, such as a jug of wine. A mule cart brings up the rear.

Temples

GREEK LIFE WAS DOMINATED by religion, so it is not surprising that the temples of ancient Greece were the biggest and most beautiful buildings. They also had a political purpose, as they were often built to celebrate civic power and pride, or to offer thanks to the patron deity of a city for success in war. Temples were made of limestone or marble with roofs and ceilings of wood. Roof tiles were made of terra-cotta or stone. Large numbers of workers must have been employed in temple construction. Huge stone blocks had to be transported from quarries in ox-drawn carts. These blocks were carved on site by masons using hammers and mallets. The tall columns were made in cylindrical sections ("drums"), lifted into position with ropes and pulleys, and held together with pegs. Decorative sculpture in the form of friezes, and statues in the pediments (the triangular gable ends), added to the grandeur and beauty of Greek temples.

CAPE SOUNION
A fifth-century marble temple to Poseidon, god of the sea, crowns a high promontory south of Athens. It was a landmark for sailors returning home to Athens. The English romantic poet George Gordon, Lord Byron (1788–1824) was very moved by its beauty.

ZEUS' TEMPLE
A great international festival of athletics (pp. 44–45) in honor of Zeus was held every four years at Olympia, a sanctuary on the banks of the Alpheios River. Colossal remains of the great temple of Zeus, built in the fifth century, and other important buildings have been found there.

TEMPLE OF CERES
Poseidonia (later called Paestum) in southern Italy, south of Naples, was a rich Greek colony and it has the best preserved archaic temples anywhere in the Greek world. This one, built in the sixth century BCE in the Doric style and known as the temple of Ceres (the Roman version of Demeter), was in fact dedicated to the goddess Athena and later used as a Christian church. For hundreds of years few people visited the site of Paestum because it was hidden by swamps and undergrowth, and this accounts for the remarkably good condition of the buildings today.

ROSETTE CAPITAL
This huge marble capital (top of a column) comes from the temple of Artemis at Ephesus in modern Turkey. An earlier temple on the same site was destroyed by fire in 356 BCE, on the same night that Alexander the Great (pp. 62–63) was born.

DORIC
The Doric style is sturdy and its top (the capital) is plain. This style was used in mainland Greece and the colonies in southern Italy and Sicily.

IONIC
The Ionic style is thinner and more elegant. Its capital is decorated with a scroll-like design (a volute). This style was found in eastern Greece and the islands.

CORINTHIAN
The Corinthian style is seldom used in the Greek world, but often seen on Roman temples. Its capital is very elaborate and decorated with acanthus leaves.

LION'S MOUTH
Rain water was sometimes drained away from the roofs of temples through spouts in the form of lions' heads. This one comes from a temple of Athena at Priene, just south of Ephesus, in modern Turkey.

COLUMNS AND CAPITALS
Most Greek buildings had vertical columns and horizontal lintels (beams). This style of construction may have been inspired by earlier wooden buildings whose roofs were supported by tree trunks.

CORINTHIAN CAPITAL
This Corinthian capital once decorated a gracious colonnaded building in Asia Minor (modern Turkey). The face is a version of a female theatrical mask. The deeply carved leaves below copy those of the acanthus plant, a favorite motif of Greek artists. The plant is easily identified by its spreading, leathery leaves.

PALMETTE ROOF TILE
The end of this roof tile is decorated with a palmette shape. It comes from a temple to Apollo at Bassae in southern Greece. This area was famous for its fighting men and Apollo may have been worshiped here as a god of soldiers.

LOTUS LEAVES
This marble fragment is crisply carved with a frieze of lotus and palmette designs and other delicate moldings. It comes from the top part of the east wall of the famous temple of the Erechtheion on the Acropolis of Athens (pp. 16–17). The roof of the south porch of the building is supported by columns in the form of standing women with baskets on their heads. Perikles ordered the construction of the Erechtheion (which survives today on the site of older buildings) in the middle fifth century BCE to beautify the city of Athens.

At home

THE GREEKS LIKED THEIR HOMES to be private. The windows were small and set high in the walls, which were made out of Sun-dried mud bricks and have not survived well. This farmhouse is a fairly simple building and townhouses would probably have had more rooms and been more luxurious. The garden or courtyard was in the middle of the house, and all the rooms were arranged around it. There might have been a well here where slave girls did the family laundry and filled the water pots. In the porch, a *herm*, a statue of the god Hermes, prevented evil spirits from entering. It is difficult to get a clear picture of a typical Greek home. This farmhouse model is based on information gathered from excavating a house to the south of Athens, which was occupied in the fourth century BCE.

Terra-cotta figurine shows a woman grinding grain to make bread

DOORS AND JARS
Wood was expensive in Greece and doors were therefore precious objects. Two bowls on stands used in wedding rituals can be seen in front.

RAIN CAT
Some rich houses had gutters on the roofs for the removal of rain water. The water flowed onto the ground through water spouts like this one, which is shaped like a lion's head.

The women's quarters (gynaeceum) housed the weaving looms, babies' cradles, and couches

Ladder to upper story

Every house had an altar, where the family would offer sacrifices to the gods

Hearth for cooking and to provide burning charcoal for portable braziers

The dining room (andron) where the men entertained their friends

ON THE TILES
Sometimes the ends of terra-cotta roof tiles in wealthier homes and in temples were decorated with human and animal faces. This gorgon head has tight curls and a protuding tongue. Originally it would have been brightly colored and clearly visible from the ground.

SITTING PRETTY
In this vase painting, a young woman, perhaps a bride preparing for her wedding, is sitting on a chair in her house. This elegant chair shape is often seen on vases.

COUCHES
As Greek couches were made mainly of wood, none have survived. This bronze decoration was once fitted onto a couch near the head rest. Similar couches were used at mealtimes.

Roof made of clay tiles

Walls made of mud bricks, sometimes plastered over

Window openings without glass but with wooden shutters

Wooden door with bronze fixtures

Porch pillars made from fallen or cut down trees on the farm land

Stone foundations were often stolen by later builders

In the country a stone wall usually surrounded the property

Women's world

Greek Woman by British artist Sir Lawrence Alma-Tadema (1836–1912)

THE LIVES OF WOMEN in ancient Greece were restricted. Women were very much under the control of their husbands, fathers, or brothers, and rarely took part in politics or any form of public life. Most women could not inherit property and were allowed very little money. A girl would marry very young, at the age of 13 or 14, and her husband, who was certain to be much older, was chosen for her by her father. The main purpose of marriage was to have a baby, preferably a boy, to carry on the male line. The status of a woman greatly increased when she had given birth to a boy (pp. 32–33). Some marriages seem to have been happy. A number of tombstones have survived that commemorate women who died in childbirth. There are tender inscriptions from the grieving husbands. It is possible that, although legally they had very little freedom, some women could make important decisions about family life. Their spinning and weaving work made an important contribution to the household.

Whorl

SPINDLE
Wool was spun into yarn with a spindle. This one is made of wood, but bronze and bone examples also exist. At one end is a weight, known as a spindle whorl. The spindle twirls around and spins the wool fiber into thread.

HOMEMAKERS
Girls in Greece did not go to school (pp. 32–33). Instead, they stayed at home and were taught by their mothers how to spin and weave and look after the house. Some wealthier women were taught to read and write. On this vase a woman is reading from a papyrus scroll.

SPINNER
On this white-ground jug a woman is spinning with both a distaff and spindle. The distaff was a shaft of wood or metal with a spike at one end and a handle at the other.

WELL WOMEN
In Athens there were public fountains where women and slave girls went to fill their water pots. Not many houses had their own private wells. The water spout is shaped like a lion's head. The women wait their turn with their water pots balanced on their heads. This was a good opportunity to meet with friends and chat.

This *epinetron* has a scene of spinning and weaving painted upon it in the black figure technique

THIGH PROTECTOR
Spinning and weaving were regarded as suitable occupations for all Greek women, even those of noble families. In preparing the wool for spinning, a woman attached a special instrument called an *epinetron* over her knee. She then rolled the wool across the surface of it and drew it out, producing thin skeins of wool.

SAPPHO
Sappho, a woman writer of the late seventh century BCE, lived on the island of Lesbos in the eastern Aegean. Women in this part of Greece seem to have had more freedom than the women of Athens, and Sappho's beautiful poems give us a glimpse of their lives and their feelings.

BEAUTY AID
Wealthy women owned many beauty aids. This bronze mirror has a stand in the form of a goddess, probably Aphrodite, holding a dove. Two little cupid figures fly on either side of her. This mirror would have been highly polished when new, so that its owner could see her reflection in it. Caskets, combs, and perfume bottles have also been found in large numbers.

The little lamps burning on the tables in front of the diners were used to light darkened rooms

ENTERTAINERS
Respectable women were expected to stay at home as much as possible, keeping house, and supervising the slaves. Only women called *hetairai* were allowed to attend the *symposia*, (banquets, pp. 36–37), an important part of Greek social life. *Hetairai* can be seen on vases playing the pipes, dancing, and generally entertaining the male banqueters. Many *hetairai* were foreigners or prisoners taken in wars.

Growing up in Greece

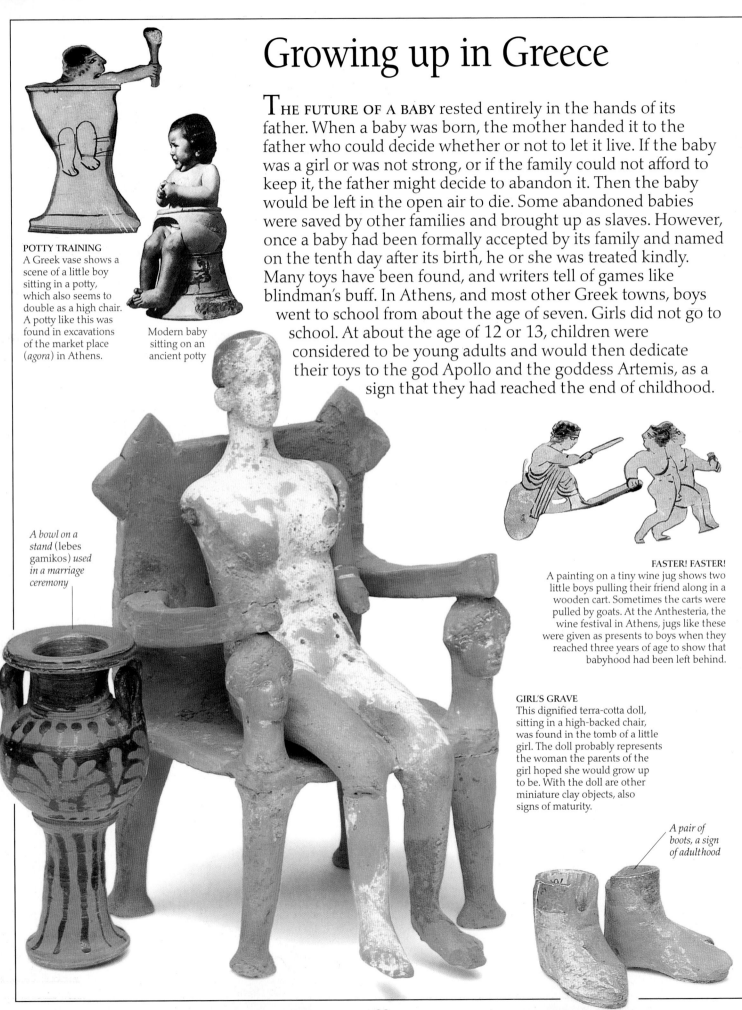

THE FUTURE OF A BABY rested entirely in the hands of its father. When a baby was born, the mother handed it to the father who could decide whether or not to let it live. If the baby was a girl or was not strong, or if the family could not afford to keep it, the father might decide to abandon it. Then the baby would be left in the open air to die. Some abandoned babies were saved by other families and brought up as slaves. However, once a baby had been formally accepted by its family and named on the tenth day after its birth, he or she was treated kindly. Many toys have been found, and writers tell of games like blindman's buff. In Athens, and most other Greek towns, boys went to school from about the age of seven. Girls did not go to school. At about the age of 12 or 13, children were considered to be young adults and would then dedicate their toys to the god Apollo and the goddess Artemis, as a sign that they had reached the end of childhood.

POTTY TRAINING
A Greek vase shows a scene of a little boy sitting in a potty, which also seems to double as a high chair. A potty like this was found in excavations of the market place (*agora*) in Athens.

Modern baby sitting on an ancient potty

A bowl on a stand (lebes gamikos) *used in a marriage ceremony*

FASTER! FASTER!
A painting on a tiny wine jug shows two little boys pulling their friend along in a wooden cart. Sometimes the carts were pulled by goats. At the Anthesteria, the wine festival in Athens, jugs like these were given as presents to boys when they reached three years of age to show that babyhood had been left behind.

GIRL'S GRAVE
This dignified terra-cotta doll, sitting in a high-backed chair, was found in the tomb of a little girl. The doll probably represents the woman the parents of the girl hoped she would grow up to be. With the doll are other miniature clay objects, also signs of maturity.

A pair of boots, a sign of adulthood

Education

When boys went to school at seven, they learned reading, writing, and arithmetic from a teacher called a *grammatistes.* They learned music, including the playing of a musical instrument, from a teacher known as a *kitharistes.* They also had to memorize poetry and learn the art of debating. Older boys might be taught by teachers called Sophists. Sophists traveled from town to town and often taught their students in the *gymnasia,* or training grounds. Girls did not go to school, but some girls from well-off families had private tutors who taught them to read and write. Their mothers taught them spinning and weaving, and how to run a home.

WAX SCRATCHER
Wooden tablets covered in wax were used in the classroom. Letters were formed in the softened wax with a stylus, usually made of bone or metal. The blunt end was used for smoothing out mistakes.

MINDER
Boys from wealthy families were taken to school by a slave called a *paidogogos,* who, on this vase, sits behind the pupil and holds a long staff. The boy stands in front of his teacher who reads from a papyrus scroll.

TRAINING FOR WAR
Traditionally, boys needed to be fit and strong so that they would grow up to be good soldiers. Therefore, there were special teachers of physical exercise called *paidotribai* (*paidotribes* in the singular). *Paidotribai* taught their pupils athletics and wrestling in the *palaistra.* This was a long low building with dressing rooms and a colonnaded courtyard covered with sand. Most Greek towns had a *palaistra.*

The *palaistra* at Olympia

CLAY COMPANY
Toys for children were often made of wood or fabric, which have not survived. Children also played with clay figurines, perhaps made by potters from leftover clay. These riders were modeled by hand, brightly painted, and then placed in the graves of children to keep them company in the afterlife.

Man riding on goose

Man riding on horse

Fun and games

RICH GREEKS, ESPECIALLY THOSE who lived in towns, had plenty of leisure time to spend talking, giving dinner parties, visiting the gymnasium, and playing all kinds of games. Music was particularly important. Greeks sang songs at births, weddings, and funerals. They had love songs, battle songs, drinking songs, and songs of thanks to the gods to celebrate the harvest. There were also many musical instruments: stringed instruments like the harp, the lyre, and the kithara (a kind of lyre), and wind instruments like the syrinx, or pan pipes, made of reeds of different lengths. Unfortunately, almost no written music has survived from ancient Greece. Perhaps we can guess what it may have sounded like by seeing the way women dance on Greek vases. They seem to be moving rhythmically to slow and haunting tunes. Greek men did not dance, but they liked to watch dancers perform at celebrations and at drinking parties (pp. 36–37). Poor Greeks, such as farmers and slaves, had very little spare time.

DANCING GIRL
This slave girl, wearing a short, pleated skirt, is dancing while playing the castanets. She is probably an entertainer at a party.

CLASH OF CYMBALS
This pair of bronze cymbals is inscribed with their owner's name, Oata. Few musical instruments like this have survived, but they can often be seen on vase paintings.

TUNEFUL TRIO
This painting from a red figure vase shows three people with their musical instruments. The woman sitting on the chair is the Muse Terpsichore. Muses were minor deities who looked after all the arts. Terpsichore seems to be concentrating hard on playing her harp, while the other two hold their lyres and listen. The man on the right is Musaios, a legendary musician.

Knucklebones

LARGE LYRE
The kithara, which this woman is playing, is a larger, wooden version of the lyre. She is plucking the strings with a plectrum, similar to those used by guitarists today. The kithara was usually played by professional musicians. This figure was made in a Greek town in southern Italy. Perhaps she is singing or chanting poetry while she plays.

BATTLES ON BOARD

Herodotos, the 5th-century Greek historian, believed that board games were invented in Lydia in Asia Minor. Counters, dice, and gaming pieces made of stone, bone, and clay have been found. Some vases show warriors playing board games while they take a rest from fighting. Here, the two Greek heroes Ajax and Achilles play a kind of backgammon or chess.

Board games similar to chutes and ladders have been known for more than 2,000 years

ON TARGET

Kottabos was a simple but popular game. It was often played at the end of a drinking party, but was not restricted to men. Players held their wine cups by one handle and flicked the dregs of wine at a target. The winner was the person who hit the target most accurately. In this charming scene, a little duck is watching a woman taking aim.

JACKS FOR JILLS

A favorite game was knucklebones. These were made from anklejoints of small, cloven-footed animals. The game was very similar to jacks and a classical author described it as being "above all a game for women."

PHYSICALLY FIT

Boys were expected to be in good physical shape and boxing was just one of many sports they were encouraged to do. Instead of gloves, ancient boxers wrapped leather thongs (*himantes*) around their hands and wrists which left their fingers free.

IN A SPIN

The top had a thread attached to it and was beaten as it spun around. A hard ground surface is needed for a really good spin.

Wining and dining

DIVER'S TOMB
A typical banqueting scene is painted on the wall of a tomb at Paestum, a Greek colony in southern Italy. It shows young men reclining together on couches, while slaves serve them with food and wine on small tables.

In Athens, and other Greek cities, men often held banquets or drinking parties (*symposia*), for their male friends. Some were small, private *symposia*, others were large-scale and public. Private *symposia* took place at home in the dining room (*andron*) which was set aside for the men's use after the evening meal. Many Greek vases show *symposia* scenes. All respectable women were excluded from a *symposion*, but slave girls called *hetairai* would entertain the men with their dancing, flute playing, and acrobatic displays (pp. 30–31). The evening began with the pouring of libations (usually wine), and the singing of special songs or hymns to the gods. The guests wore garlands and perfume. Early in the evening they might discuss politics and philosophy, but as they drank more and more wine, they would tell each other jokes, riddles, and stories. Eventually, after drinking a lot of wine, the banqueters would fall asleep on their comfortable couches, leaving the women and slave boys to clean up.

DRINKING CUP
This is a special kind of drinking cup used at a *symposion*. It is in the form of a ram's head and the rim is painted with a banqueting scene of guests leaning back on cushioned couches. It gives us a clear impression of the elegant and comfortable life-style that wealthy Athenian men enjoyed. The cup has no base so was probably passed around from hand to hand.

Olives are plentiful in Greece and bowls of olives, both green and black, would be offered at a *symposion,* possibly as an appetizer

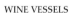

WINE VESSELS
Wine was the Greeks' favorite drink. It was drunk by everybody, not just the rich, and was nearly always diluted with water. Bread dipped in wine, eaten with a few figs, was a typical Greek breakfast. Many different kinds of wine container have survived. These are often made of clay, but sometimes of bronze. The big bronze vessel on the far left was used for mixing water and wine together. The mixture would have been transferred to the jug with the ladle and the slave would fill his master's cup.

FARE FIT FOR THE GODS
The Greeks grew wheat and barley to make bread and porridge, which were an important part of their diet. Lentils, peas, onions, garlic, and cabbage were also eaten in large quantities. Meat was eaten mainly on sacrificial occasions such as religious festivals, when the sacrificial animal would be shared out among the worshipers.
For the rest of the time, fish and cheese were the main source of protein. Fruit such as pomegranates, figs, apples, and pears was available; oranges and lemons were not cultivated in Greece until a much later date.

Even people who lived in towns kept a family goat which provided milk and cheese.

Bread and goat's cheese

FISH DISH
A variety of fish might be served at a *symposion*. Many Greek towns were near the sea and fishermen went out in boats to catch mullet, tuna, mackerel, and sturgeon. This mackerel is on a bed of bay leaves. The Greeks liked to flavor their food with fresh herbs.

Figs in a modern dish

Squid

Mackerel in bay leaves in a modern platter

SWEETENERS
The combination of summer drought, winter rains, and long spells of winter sunshine is ideal for long-germinating plants such as the fig. In the absence of sugar, sweet fruits like figs were very popular as a dessert. Honey was used in cakes and cookies.

FRUITS OF THE SEA
Octopus and squid are abundant in the seas around Greece, and fish was a staple of everyone's diet. Seafood still plays a large part in Greek cuisine today.

A day out

GREEK THEATERS ARE AMONG the most spectacular buildings that survive from ancient times. In cities like Athens, or at sacred sites like Delphi and Epidauros, people flocked to see dramas in honor of the gods. In Athens, performances for the wine god Dionysus developed into what are now known as plays. From the middle of the sixth century BCE, these plays were organized as dramatic competitions and were put on during the spring festival of Dionysus. By the fifth century BCE, both tragedies and comedies were performed, and many have survived to the present time. Audiences in Athens spent days watching the plays, seated in the theater of Dionysus on the slope of the Acropolis. The actors were all men, taking the female parts as well, and no more than three main actors could speak to each other at one time. A larger group of actors, the chorus, commented on the play's action and addressed the audience more directly. Music accompanied the plays, which were acted out on a flat circular area called the *orchestra*. Women were probably not allowed to go to the theater at all.

TIRED OUT
This small terra-cotta figure shows a comic actor dressed as an old woman. He wears a mask with a wrinkled face and crinkly hair, which he has pushed back on his head, as he rests wearily on a seat.

EURIPIDES
The expression on this sculpture reflects the serious subjects dealt with by the Athenian playwright Euripides. Some of his plays dealt with the horrors of war, and upset the Athenians because they hinted at Athens' savage treatment of her enemies.

BIRD'S EYE VIEW
From high up in the back row at Epidauros you can get a clear view of the performance. Here, a temporary set has been built for the modern production of a play.

EPIDAUROS
This ground-level view of the 14,000 seat theater at Epidauros gives an idea of what it is like to be an actor going into the performing area. The carefully curved auditorium (*theatron* or viewing theater) is a huge semicircular bowl cut into the surface of the hillside. Its shape is not just designed for excellent viewing; sound, too, is caught and amplified, and actors speaking in the *orchestra* can be heard in the back row.

SOPHOKLES

Portraits of famous playwrights were produced some time after their death, so they were not true likenesses. But these sculptures honored the memory of great writers like the playwright Sophokles. This print decorates a 19th-century text of the plays. Sophokles' plays about royal or legendary families and their tragic lives, like those of King Oedipus or Electra, daughter of Agamemnon, still grip audiences today.

GREEK DRAMA ALIVE AND WELL
A group of actors from Britain's Royal National Theatre perform three plays called *The Oresteia,* by the Athenian playwright Aeschylus. They tell of the death of Agamemnon after the Trojan war and how his son Orestes avenged him.

The very elaborate hat is a sign that this bearded man's wealth was not acquired honestly

The muse holds a mask portraying a young woman, one of the characters in Greek comedy from the fourth century BCE.

SOUVENIR STATUETTES
Statuettes in terra-cotta, originally painted in bright colors, are perhaps souvenirs of theater visits. Sets of the entire casts of plays have been found in graves. The graceful female figure is probably a muse, one of the nine guardians of the arts in Greek mythology. The terra-cotta of the bearded actor represents a sinister figure from later Greek comedy, who lived off the earnings of *hetairai*.

Body beautiful

BEAUTY AND CLEANLINESS were important to the ancient Greeks. In sculpture and on vases, both men and women can be seen wearing elegant, softly folded garments and standing in graceful poses (pp. 42–43). Young men took great care of their bodies, keeping them fit and strong so that they could be good soldiers and athletes. Nudity was considered quite normal for young men who always competed naked at their Games (pp. 44–45). After exercise, men and boys rubbed themselves with olive oil to keep their skin supple. Women kept their whole bodies clothed, and wore something on their heads when they went out. Their clothes were so finely spun, however, that they were sometimes almost transparent, and must have been light and cool to wear in the hot summer. Women wore perfumed oils and tried to keep out of the sun as much as possible, because a sun tan was not considered beautiful. Wealthy women owned jewelry, much of it in gold and silver and very ornate.

DECORATION IN DEATH
Jewelry was an indication of wealth and prosperity. On this grave relief, a slave is shown handing a bracelet to a woman, probably the dead person herself.

THE AEGINA TREASURE
This gold earring is one of a pair that was found, with a pendant, on the island of Aegina. It was made in Minoan times (pp. 8–9). The circular shape is a snake, and inside it are two dogs standing on the heads of monkeys.

FOLLOWER OF FASHION
This terra-cotta figurine shows a fashionable Greek woman (pp. 42–43) wearing a tunic (*chiton*) and cloak (*himation*). She is holding a kind of fan. Clothes were often brightly colored, as can be seen from the traces of paint which remain on the statuette. Hairstyles were very elaborate, and this woman is wearing some kind of head decoration. Many figures like this have been found at Tanagra in central Greece.

POWDER POT
Women used a special round, flat pot, called a *pyxis*, to hold their perfumes and cosmetics. These pots were sometimes decorated with scenes of women spinning and weaving.

BATHTIME
Greeks bathed very regularly. This terra-cotta shows that tubs were smaller than most modern ones. At the feet end of this tub, there was a hollow where the water was deeper so that the woman could splash it backward over her body.

Silver *fibulae*

HEADDRESS
Beautiful gold wreaths and sprays sometimes decorated the heads of statues of gods and goddesses that were carried in procession at festivals. Occasionally, wreaths were placed on the heads of corpses in tombs.

ELEGANT EARS
Most earrings were made of gold or silver and were made for pierced ears. These are in the shape of little boats with cockleshells hanging from them. Inside the boats are tiny sirens, half-bird, half-female creatures.

The Westmacott athlete

IDEAL ATHLETE
This statue is a Roman copy of a Greek bronze by the famous Greek sculptor, Polykleitos. He liked to make statues of naked male athletes because he was interested in the ideal proportions and measurements of the male body. At the site of Olympia there is a statue base to which the original Greek figure may have belonged, because the holes in the base for the feet are exactly the right shape and size. The base is inscribed with the name of a young boxer called Kyniskos.

SILVER MEDALLION
This silver medallion may once have been part of the decoration on a bowl. It shows a girl offering a gift to Aphrodite, the goddess of beauty. Aphrodite sits on a rock decorated with flowers and is turning to look at Eros, who is playfully putting an upturned basket on his head. Around the medallion are a pair of silver brooches (*fibulae*) linked together by a long plaited silver chain. This might have been used for fastening a cloak.

PERFUME POT
This brightly colored glass bottle was probably used for perfume. Most perfume pots were made of clay and hundreds of them have been found. Scent made in Corinth and Rhodes was exported in the bottles to other countries.

WELL-OILED
On this vase painting, an athlete rubs his friend's back with olive oil. Afterward he removes the surplus oil with a curved bronze body scraper.

Clothes for comfort

GREEK CLOTHES WERE MADE largely of wool provided by local sheep. The wool was spun very finely so that garments were thinner than modern woolen clothing. Lighter, linen clothes made out of spun flax were also worn. Very wealthy people bought expensive silks from the East, and in Hellenistic times, mulberry trees were planted on the island of Kos to start a local silk industry. Bright colors were popular, especially among women. Purple was obtained from sea snails, and a violet shade from an insect larva called the kermes worm. Other dyes came from plants. Poorer people probably wore undyed clothes. The shapes of clothes were similar for both men and women and hardly changed over hundreds of years. The basic dress was a straight tunic fastened at the shoulder with brooches or pins, with a cloak flung over the top.

LADY HAMILTON
Sir William Hamilton, British Ambassador to Naples in the late 18th century, was a collector of Greek antiquities. His wife Emma, famous for her liaison with Lord Nelson, often dressed in Greek costume.

HAIR DRESSING
Greek women (except slave women) wore their hair long. This woman's style was fashionable in the Classical period. The hair is piled up at the back of the head and held in place with a net and ribbons. Diadems, and other gold hair decorations, were worn on special occasions.

READY TO WEAR
The *chiton* was said to have been invented in the East Greek region of Ionia. It was made from a single rectangle of cloth, cut into two and fastened at intervals from neck to elbows to give a graceful loose sleeve effect. It was gathered at the waist with a belt. The *chiton* shown here is made out of modern woolen fabric. This is perhaps slightly thicker and fuller than the original material would have been in the fifth century BCE. Another earlier kind of *chiton*, sometimes called a *peplos*, originated in mainland Greece. It was secured with big pins on the shoulders and did not have sleeves.

Chiton

WRAP UP
Greek underwear was not fitted, but, like outer clothes, was wrapped around the body. On this vase a woman wearing a strip of material as a bra is putting her *chiton* over her head.

Chiton

GREEK FANTASY
Sir Lawrence Alma-Tadema (pp. 30–31) often chose classical subjects for his paintings. The architecture and clothing, however, frequently owed more to his imagination than to historical accuracy.

MEN'S WEAR

This man is wearing a tunic, the *chiton*, and a cloak, the *himation*. His *chiton* has been pulled up over his belt. Workmen nearly always wore a very short *chiton* to give them greater freedom of movement. Over the top this man is wearing a rectangular *himation*. Younger men sometimes wore only the *himation*, which was draped over one shoulder and wrapped around the hips. Greek clothes did not have hems because they were woven to the correct length.

Woolen chiton

Woolen himation

FAMILY GROUP

Children wore similar clothes to their parents, but probably had short tunics so that they could run around easily. Adults and children went barefoot indoors and put on leather sandals with many straps when they went out.

SUN PROTECTION

Outside, both men and women wore hats to protect themselves from the hot sun. Women thought a suntan was unattractive, and if they did not have a hat they would pull their cloaks up over their heads to shield their faces, or would wear a veil called a *kredemnon*. A wide-brimmed traveling hat, like the one worn here by this fashionable young man, was called a *petasos*. It was made of wool, but hats made of fox fur and straw were also common. This youth is wearing a short traveling cloak called a *chlamys*, fastened on the shoulder with a pin or brooch.

The Greek games

THE GREEKS BELIEVED IN THE VALUE of sport as training for warfare, and as a way of honoring the gods. There were many local sporting competitions, but four big athletic festivals attracted men from all over the Greek world. Of these, the most important was the Olympic Games, held every four years in honor of Zeus at Olympia. Success in the Games brought honor to the athlete's family and to his hometown. Some successful athletes acquired almost mythical status. Wars were suspended to allow people to travel in safety to and from Olympia. Many beautiful temples and other buildings which provided facilities for athletes and spectators have been excavated there. The Games went on into Roman times, coming to an end late in the fourth century. In Athens, there were also four-yearly games (Panathenaic Games) held in honor of Athena as part of her religious festival, and they were an important public holiday. Discipline in sport was strict, and breaking the rules was punished severely.

TRAINING TIME
Wrestling, although popular, was regarded as one of the most dangerous of Greek sports. Tripping your opponent up was permitted but biting or gouging out his eyes was strictly forbidden. The man on the left of this statue base is in a racing start position, and the man on the right is testing his javelin.

PRIZE POTS
This boxing scene (336 BCE) was painted on a special kind of olive oil pot given as a prize to victorious athletes at the festival of Athena in Athens. Known as Panathenaic vases, they always had a painting of Athena on one side and a painting of the event on the other. Here, two boxers with rippling muscles are fighting each other. Instead of boxing gloves, they wear leather thongs wrapped around their fists.

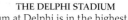

THE DELPHI STADIUM
The stadium at Delphi is in the highest part of the ancient city. The stone starting grooves on the track survive, as well as many of the seats, especially where they were cut into the mountainside. The stadium could hold 7,000 spectators.

THE OLYMPIC SPIRIT
The spirit of the Olympic Games has greatly inspired artists. This 19th-century German duotone depicts naked athletes exercising against a background of classical columns.

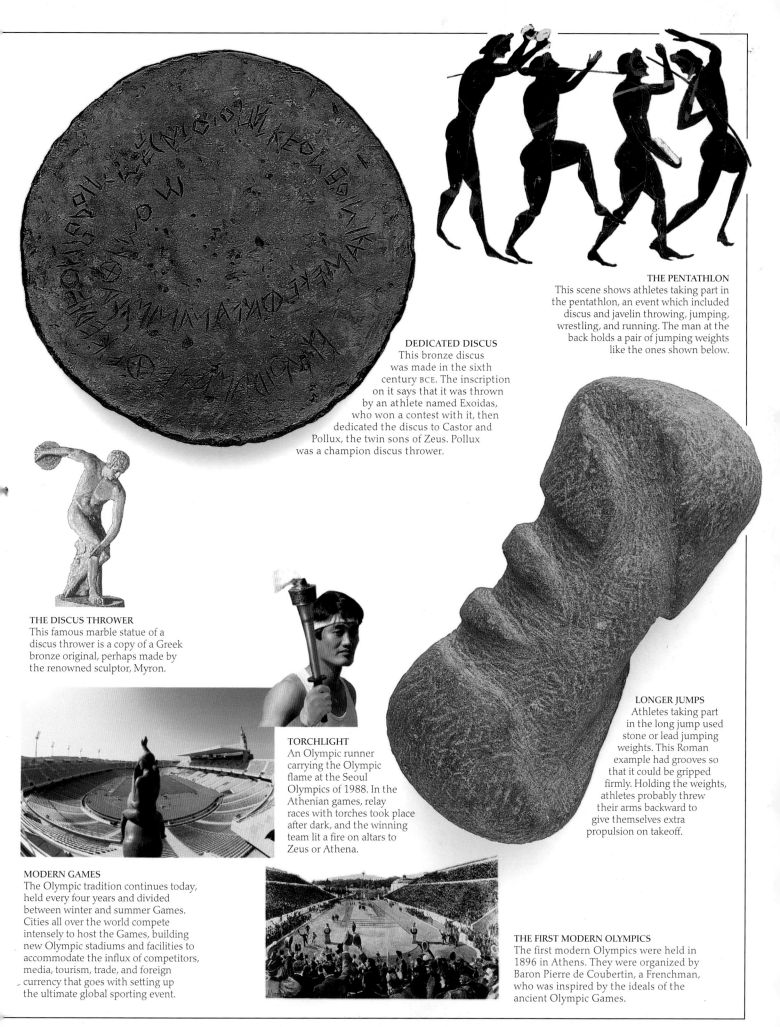

THE PENTATHLON
This scene shows athletes taking part in the pentathlon, an event which included discus and javelin throwing, jumping, wrestling, and running. The man at the back holds a pair of jumping weights like the ones shown below.

DEDICATED DISCUS
This bronze discus was made in the sixth century BCE. The inscription on it says that it was thrown by an athlete named Exoidas, who won a contest with it, then dedicated the discus to Castor and Pollux, the twin sons of Zeus. Pollux was a champion discus thrower.

THE DISCUS THROWER
This famous marble statue of a discus thrower is a copy of a Greek bronze original, perhaps made by the renowned sculptor, Myron.

TORCHLIGHT
An Olympic runner carrying the Olympic flame at the Seoul Olympics of 1988. In the Athenian games, relay races with torches took place after dark, and the winning team lit a fire on altars to Zeus or Athena.

LONGER JUMPS
Athletes taking part in the long jump used stone or lead jumping weights. This Roman example had grooves so that it could be gripped firmly. Holding the weights, athletes probably threw their arms backward to give themselves extra propulsion on takeoff.

MODERN GAMES
The Olympic tradition continues today, held every four years and divided between winter and summer Games. Cities all over the world compete intensely to host the Games, building new Olympic stadiums and facilities to accommodate the influx of competitors, media, tourism, trade, and foreign currency that goes with setting up the ultimate global sporting event.

THE FIRST MODERN OLYMPICS
The first modern Olympics were held in 1896 in Athens. They were organized by Baron Pierre de Coubertin, a Frenchman, who was inspired by the ideals of the ancient Olympic Games.

Wisdom and beauty

For the Greeks, philosophy, or the "love of wisdom," was something that involved not just the way people lived, but a great deal of science as well. Early thinkers were concerned with ideas about the physical world. Heraclitus developed a theory involving atoms, and Pythagoras came up with his theorem as part of his view that the world was based on mathematical patterns. He and his fellow thinkers, both men and women, also believed that souls could be reborn in other bodies (reincarnation), and some even thought that beans might contain the souls of old friends and therefore shouldn't be eaten. Philosophy and the arts were part of religion, too. Religious hymns celebrated the meaning and mystery of life and explained the origin of the gods. The Greeks made handsome objects both as offerings to the gods and also for their own sakes. Music, sculpture, painting, pottery, and dance all thrived in ancient Greece.

ROYAL PUPIL
Greek philosophers were at the center of Greek life. Here, the philosopher Aristotle is tutoring the young prince, Alexander of Macedon (pp. 62–63).

PIPED MUSIC
This pipe from Athens, made of sycamore wood, is one of a pair; Greeks played sets of double pipes. There was originally a reed in the mouthpiece, so the pipes would have sounded a bit like a modern oboe.

Pythagoras holding the cosmos

VASE PAINTER
Vase painting is considered to be one of the minor arts, but the work of the potter and painter Exekias was of a very high standard. This exquisitely painted drinking cup shows the god Dionysus reclining in a boat, with his special plant, the vine, twining around the mast. The god, like the vine, was believed to have come from the east. The dolphins may be the pirates who tried to capture him, now turned into sea creatures.

ANIMAL AMPLIFIER
The European tortoise was once plentiful in Greece, and its empty shell made an excellent soundbox for the stringed instrument called the lyre. Its strings, which were plucked with a plectrum (pick), could be tightened to produce a range of notes.

THE KEY TO THE COSMOS
Pythagoras (c.580–500 BCE), originally from the island of Samos, was the leading light of a group of religious thinkers in southern Italy. They believed that the key to the world (cosmos) lay in numbers and mathematical relationships.

SEEING EYE TO EYE
The eye was an important symbol in ancient Greece. It gave life and power to objects. Statues had their eyes painted in; eyes on the front of warships magically guided them. This eye cup of the sixth century BCE blends the elements of a face with the patterns found on many wine cups. The eyebrows are echoed by long strands of ivy, a plant associated with Dionysus. A pair of his satyr friends are escaping around the sides of the cup. The eyes themselves have perfectly formed circles incised with a sharp-pointed tool..

Cup has no flat base and was probably handed around from hand to hand

DEATH BY HEMLOCK
Socrates' teachings were so astonishing, even for the fairly broad-minded Athenians, that some people became suspicious of him. He was accused of corrupting the minds of the young, and of showing disrespect for the gods. He was imprisoned, then made to take his own life by drinking a poison, hemlock.

FOUNDING FATHERS
Side by side, with proud gestures, philosophers Aristotle (384–322 BCE) and Plato (427–347 BCE) are outlined against the sky, each holding one of their major books in their hands. The Italian artist Raphael (1483–1520), has placed them in the very center of his fresco, painted on the wall of a great room in the Vatican in the early 16th century.

WORD OF MOUTH
Although Socrates (469–399 BCE) is one of the most famous of the ancient Greek philosophers, he produced no philosophical writings. He explored philosophy by discussing it intently, often pretending to be ignorant of a subject in order to allow his opponents to demolish their own case unintentionally. Socrates has a bare chest in this marble statuette; philosophers were often shown dressed in this way.

PLATO AND PUPILS
The leading philosophers attracted groups of pupils, and much teaching was done in discussion groups. Plato set up a school for philosophers in Athens, his native city, in a pleasant garden called the Academy. Plato wrote up many ideas of Socrates in the form of "dialogues," or discussions, between pupils and teachers.

Vases and vessels

Black-figure vase

THE BEST GREEK POTTERY was made in Athens. A high-quality clay was found there which fired well to a beautiful reddish-brown color. Athenian potters worked in a potters' quarter called the *Kerameikos*. They produced huge quantities of wheel-made pottery for use at home and for the export market. There are various styles of decoration in vase painting. Between 1000 and 700 BCE geometric patterns were the fashion. Gradually, around 720 BCE, oriental motifs came into fashion. The black-figure technique—black silhouette figures painted in a highly refined clay solution on the reddish clay background—was the main way of decorating pots from the early to mid sixth century BCE. Inner details were incised with a bone or metal tool. Soon after 500 BCE, the red-figure technique took over. The figures of gods and animals were now left in the reddish-brown clay and instead the background was painted in with a clay solution which, in the firing process, turned black. Many vases have been preserved in excellent condition.

DRINKING UP TIME
Special drinking cups in the form of animal heads were very popular. This angry-looking griffin *rhyton* is a good example. The wine would have spilled if the *rhyton* were put down, so perhaps it was passed from person to person until all the wine was gone.

FIRST SIP
Trefoil top

This miniature wine jug is called a *chous*. It shows two schoolboys, one reading from a papyrus scroll and the other holding a lyre. The jug would have been filled with wine and given to a little boy as a special present at the festival of Dionysus, god of wine.

WHAT A BOAR!
Stories of the 12 labors of Herakles often appeared on vases (pp. 22–23). On this black-figure vase, Herakles holds the Erymanthian boar above King Eurystheus, who cowers in a jar.

The purplish-red color is a mixture of the black clay solution and a red iron oxide

COLLECTOR'S ITEM
This early 19th-century cartoon shows Sir William Hamilton (pp. 42–43), caricatured as a water pot (*hydria*). Sir William was a great expert on and collector of Greek art, especially vases.

VASE VAULT
In this engraving, Sir William is supervising the opening of a tomb in Italy. The skeleton is surrounded by vases which were exported from Athens.

VASE SHAPES
Vases were made in different shapes according to their different uses.

Storage containers for oil or wine

AMPHORA PELIKE HYDRIA

Pots in which to mix wine and water

CALYX-KRATER VOLUTE-KRATER BELL-KRATER DINOS

Jugs for pouring wine

OINOCHOE OLPE OINOCHOE OLPE

Drinking cups

KYLIX SKYPHOS KANTHAROS RHYTON

Perfume, oil, and cosmetic containers

PYXIS LEKYTHOS SQUAT LEKYTHOS ALABASTRON

A lion killing a stag

Water pot

SPHINX
This vase incorporates a clay figure of a sphinx, part woman, part lion. As well as being a beautiful table decoration, it also served a useful function. Wine was poured in at the top, and drained down through a hole in the bottom into a smaller cup. By this method, air was introduced into the wine, which made it taste better.

Grazing horse painted in outline with interior markings

SCENT FROM CORINTH
This perfume pot (*aryballos*) was made in Corinth, a town which produced novelty perfume pots in curious shapes and exported them all over the Mediterranean. The pot would have had a wax stopper to prevent the evaporation of the perfume.

GRIFFIN
This extraordinary jug has a spout in the form of a griffin's head. Made on one of the Greek islands in the seventh century BCE, it is painted with scenes influenced by the art of the east.

Decorated interior

LOOK! TWO HANDS!
This drinking cup (*kylix*) was held by both handles when in use. It was painted in the fifth century BCE in the red-figure technique. The exterior decoration could be admired when the cup was hung on the wall by one handle.

NO CHANGE
A modern potter is handpainting a vase. The ancient techniques are still in use today. Good copies of ancient vases can be bought.

49

Farming, fishing, and food

LIFE ON A GREEK FARM was difficult, as the soil in much of Greece is of poor quality. Greek farmers plowed in spring and then again in the fall. Plows, which were pulled by oxen, were made of wood and sometimes tipped with iron to make them sharper. The farmworker followed the plow, scattering seed, such as barley, by hand. Farmers prayed to Zeus, and Demeter, goddess of the grain, for a wonderful harvest. On the slopes of the hills there were vineyards and some picked grapes drying in the sun. Other grapes were gathered to make wine, the most popular Greek drink. Most towns and villages were near the sea, and a variety of fish was caught using bronze fish hooks. Wealthy people hunted wild deer, boar, and hare. Poorer people ate meat only on special festival occasions when animals were sacrificed to the gods and then shared out among the worshipers.

DINNER SERVICE
Wealthy people always ate and drank while reclining on a couch. Slaves would bring in food and place it on a small table in front of the diner. This bronze banqueter is said to have come from Dodona in northwestern Greece.

TIME STANDS STILL
This shepherd and flock going home for the night look the same as they would have in ancient times.

The hunter with his dog and prey is taken from a vase

The fisherman with his catch appears on a Cretan fresco

HUNTING AND FISHING
This fresco of a Bronze Age fisherman comes from Santorini, a volcanic island near Crete. Perhaps he was bringing the fish as an offering to the palace there. The hunter (a vase painting) is carrying a fox and a hare, while his hunting dog runs beside him. He would not have eaten the fox, but might have made a warm hat from the fur.

FISH DISH
This dish is painted with fish and other sea creatures and was probably used for the fish course at a dinner party. The hollow in the center was filled with a thick sauce into which the diner would dip his fish before eating it.

BEASTS OF BURDEN
Donkeys were used to take produce to market and for transportation. Their hardiness was ideal for a rough terrain. These two little clay donkeys were toys.

Large fish being carried to market

The donkey's rider is sitting on some cheeses

Duck's head decorates the end of the strainer

SWIMMING IN OIL
This little dolphin skimming over the waves is an oil container, used in food preparation. Dolphins were common in the waters off Greece.

FINE WINE
Wine was the most popular Greek drink, enjoyed at all times of the day. It was quite thick, needed to be strained, and was nearly always diluted with water. This wine strainer is made of bronze. Many different utensils and containers were used for the storing, serving, and drinking of wine.

ATTIC OIL
Attica, the region around Athens, was famous for its olive groves. Olive oil was used in cooking, washing, and lighting.

OLIVE HARVEST
Olive trees grow abundantly in Greece. On this vase, four people are gathering olives. One is sitting up in the tree, two are shaking the branches with sticks, and, on the ground below, another is gathering the fallen olives in a basket.

Dregs collected in the bottom of the strainer

Fossilized snail on egg

GOAT FOR ALL SEASONS
Goats were very useful animals. They required only rough grazing and their skins provided warm clothing for country people in winter, as well as milk and cheese. This little bronze goat was made about 500 BCE.

EGG CUP
Five hen's eggs in a terra-cotta cup were found in a tomb on the island of Rhodes. They are over 2,000 years old. Many households kept hens, and eggs were an important part of the daily diet. Funeral offerings of eggs, both real like these or stone or clay imitations, were common in Greek graves. They seem to have been symbols of life after death.

Crafts, travel, and trade

STONE CARVERS, METALWORKERS, jewelers, shoemakers, and many other craftsmen flourished in the cities of Greece. Their workshops were usually in the center of town around the *agora*, or marketplace. People would come to buy their products, and farmers from the countryside would sell their vegetables, fruit, and cheese. There were also weights-and-measures officials, money-changers, acrobats, dancers, and slaves standing on platforms waiting for a buyer. Most ordinary people did not travel far from home (except to war). There were few good roads, and the faithful donkey was the most reliable form of transportation for shorter journeys. If a Greek wanted to travel a long distance he would usually go by boat around the coast, thereby avoiding the mountains that cover much of the country. There was a great deal of trade between the city-states and the Greek colonies, as well as with other Mediterranean countries. Oil, wine, pottery, and metal work were the main exports.

FISHY BUSINESS
Fishing provides a livelihood for many Greeks today just as it did in ancient times. A modern fisherman on the island of Mykonos is mending his nets.

TEMPLE TREASURE
This clay jug with coins was found in the foundations of the temple of Artemis at Ephesus. The coins, made of electrum, probably date from 650–625 BCE. This was soon after coinage was introduced into Greece from Lydia in Asia Minor (roughly, modern Turkey) where coins were invented.

Coin showing the infant Herakles strangling snakes

THREE COINS
Each city-state, as a symbol of independence, issued its own coins which were at first made of electrum (an alloy of gold and silver), and later solely of silver, or occasionally gold. They were often beautifully decorated with the symbols of Greek deities, and many modern coins have been modeled on them.

Coin showing Cyrus, the king of Persia

A tortoise coin from the island of Aegina

INTO AFRICA
This pot in the form of the head of an African is evidence of the widespread trading contacts of the Greeks. Like most ancient sailors, they preferred to keep the coast within sight where possible.

BEASTS OF BURDEN
Donkeys could negotiate narrow mountain tracks and could carry heavy burdens. They still do today.

SHOEMAKER
This shoemaker is depicted at the bottom of a red-figure cup. He is bending over strips of leather which he is cutting and shaping. Boots, sandals, and tools hang from the wall above him. This scene would have become visible to the drinker when he had drained his cup.

AT THE LOOM
Upright looms, just like this one in use today, were used by women in classical times to make woolen clothing, drapes, and furnishing fabrics. Weaving was regarded as a noble as well as a necessary task.

BLACKSMITH
This painting on a jug shows a blacksmith at work. His furnace is a brick-built shaft fueled with charcoal. Bellows would have been used to fan the flames. The metal, which was placed inside the shaft, trickled down to form a lump at the bottom, which the blacksmith can here be seen removing with a pair of tongs.

POTTER
The Greeks are famous for their beautiful pottery. Every town had its potters' quarter (pp. 48–49) where pots were made and sold. On this wine cup, a potter sits at his wheel, the speed of which he controls with his knee. Above him on a shelf are some of his pots, and below him (now slightly damaged) sits a pet dog who is watching his master at work.

DEEP SEA FISHING
A great variety of fish were available in the deeper waters. Wooden vessels, like this modern one, were used for such fishing expeditions. Eels and salted fish were favorite Greek delicacies.

Warfare

SHIELDED
This Greek vase painting shows how the soldier wears his shield, passing his arm under an iron bar and gripping a leather strap at the rim.

WARFARE WAS a normal part of Greek life, and the city-states frequently fought each other. Many Greek men, therefore, had to join an army, and from the earliest times had to pay for their own armor and equipment. In Athens, boys trained as soldiers between the ages of 18 and 20, after which they could be called up for military service. In Sparta, it was much earlier (pp. 56–57). Athenian soldiers were led by ten commanders called *strategoi*. The infantry soldiers were the backbone of the Greek armies and they fought in close formations called phalanxes. Poorer soldiers served in auxiliary units as archers and stone-slingers. When laying siege to cities, the armies of Hellenistic Greece used catapults, flame-throwers, battering rams, and cauldrons containing burning coals and sulfur. Athens controlled its empire by means of oar-powered warships or triremes. At the height of its power, Athens could rely on about 300 triremes.

Helmet with nose protection

Body armor

Greaves

HOPLITE
Greek soldiers were called hoplites from the word *hoplon* meaning shield. Only men from wealthy families could be hoplites, because only they could afford expensive armor and weapons.

BATTLE OF SALAMIS
The famous sea battle of Salamis was a turning point in the Persian Wars (pp. 18–19). It took place just off the coast of Athens in 480 BCE and was a triumphant victory for the Greeks over the Persian fleet. As a result of this battle, the Persian king Xerxes and much of his army went back to Asia, abandoning the invasion of Greece.

SPEEDY BEASTS
Greek chariots were often decorated with animals associated with speed. These bronze horses were once fixed on to a fast chariot.

NAKED BRAVERY
In this painted scene from a vase, a warrior is holding a metal cuirass, (body armor). He also has a long spear and a shield. Nakedness is a symbol of heroic bravery in Greek art.

FOOT COMBAT
A painted vase shows two Greek combatants separated by a herald.

HELMETS
Helmets protected the head from every sort of slash and from blows and knocks. They varied in shape and some had crests made of horse hair to make the wearer appear more impressive and frightening.

Attic helmet has no nose guard

Corinthian helmet with long nose-piece and cheek guards

BREASTPLATE
The breastplate, or cuirass, was usually, although not always, made of bronze. It was the main piece of body armor protecting all the upper organs. Cuirasses were made to measure, each man being specially fitted. More expensive cuirasses would have ridges, roughly aligned to the body muscles, which were meant to deflect blows. The cuirass was made of two plates joined at the sides by leather straps. The side areas, therefore, were the most vulnerable parts of the body.

Sculpted ridges roughly aligning with chest muscles

GREAVES
Hoplites wore bronze leg guards called greaves (below) to protect the lower part of their legs in battle. Some of these greaves may have originally been fixed on to large statues of heroic warriors in southern Italy.

WARSHIP
The fastest Greek ship was called a trireme and it needed 170 oarsmen to row it. They sat in three levels, one above the other, on either side of the boat. At the prow was a pointed ram strengthened with metal, which could sink enemy ships. There was often an eye painted on the prow (pp. 46–47). This illustration shows two sails, but warships may have had only one, probably made of linen and lowered when the ship was engaged in battle.

The long spear was the main weapon of the Greek infantry

CHAMPION FIGHT
This red-figure vase shows a fight between two heroes of the Trojan War, Achilles and Hektor (pp. 12–13). The vase painter has clearly painted the blood flowing from the wound just above Hektor's knee. Both heroes are wearing the crested helmets and armor worn by infantry soldiers of the 5th century BCE.

The state of Sparta

SPARTA IN SOUTHERN GREECE WAS FOUNDED in the tenth century BCE by the Dorians, who defeated the original inhabitants of the area. Two centuries later, Sparta conquered its neighbor, Messenia, and gained excellent agricultural land. It became a luxury-loving state producing fine crafts. Music and poetry also flourished. Later, the Spartans were defeated in war, and the conquered Messenians engaged in a long-running rebellion, so Sparta turned to military matters. It became a superpower in Greece and the main rival of Athens, and Spartan society was dominated by the need to maintain power. All men of Spartan birth had to serve in the army. Their whole lives were dedicated to learning the arts of war. Boys of seven were taken from their families to live in army barracks. Non-citizens in Sparta were either *perioikoi* or *helots*. The *perioikoi* were free men who, although they did not have the rights of citizens, were allowed to trade, and serve in the army. *Helots* were the descendants of the original inhabitants of the area. They farmed the land and did all the heavy work for their Spartan overlords.

HARBOUR BATTLE
The Piraeus is the port of Athens, 4 miles (6 km) to the southwest of the city. In this engraving it is being besieged by Spartan ships in 388 BCE.

NATURAL PROTECTION
This 19th-century German engraving shows the site of Sparta in a fertile plain of Lakonia in southern Greece. Its remoteness was an advantage to the warring Spartans and the high mountains to the east, north, and west, and the sea to the south, formed natural defenses.

SPARTAN WARRIOR
The Greek historian Herodotus wrote that Spartan soldiers, like this one of the fifth century BCE, always combed their long hair when they felt they might be about to put their lives at risk, as when going into battle. The scarlet color of the military cloaks became a symbol of Spartan pride.

THE YOUNG SPARTANS
Spartan scenes were a popular subject with artists of the 19th century. This unusual painting by French impressionist painter Edgar Degas (1834–1917) shows boys and girls exercising in the valley of the Eurotas River, which runs through Sparta. The girls look much more aggressive than girls from other Greek cities.

SPARTAN REGIME
The Spartan system of education, with its emphasis on physical fitness, was much admired in 19th-century England. Corporal punishment was regarded as character-forming for schoolboys, just as it was in ancient Sparta. The violence of this cartoon by British cartoonist George Cruikshank (1792–1878) suggests that he thought otherwise.

OFFERINGS

Hundreds of thousands of small figurines have been found at a sanctuary of Artemis Orthia on the banks of the Eurotas River at Sparta. Among animals such as stags, dogs, and horses are representations of Artemis herself. There are also figurines of the goddess Athena wearing a helmet. The figurines were made at the sanctuary and sold to visitors who often left them behind as offerings to the goddess. It was to this sanctuary that Spartan boys were taken to be whipped as a demonstration of their toughness and endurance.

Artemis

Warrior

Artemis

Figure playing pipes

IN THE LEAD

This girl is taking part in a running race and is looking back to see how far she is in the lead. She is wearing a very short skirt, which no girl from any other Greek city would dare to wear. Girls did not fight in wars but, like most boys, they were trained in running and for an outdoor life. This made them fit and strong so that they would have healthy babies who would grow up to be good soldiers.

A stag

Science and medicine

ASCLEPIADES
Asclepiades was a famous Greek doctor of the first century BCE. He was very knowledgeable in the theory and practice of medicine. He also believed in wine as an aid to recovery and the importance of a pleasant bedside manner, so he was very popular with all his patients.

THE GREEKS WERE INTERESTED in science and, influenced by Egyptian and Babylonian scholars, made advances in biology, mathematics, astronomy, and geography. In the third century BCE, the astronomer, Aristarchus, already understood that the Earth revolved around the Sun, and another astronomer, Anaxagoras (500–428 BCE), discovered that the Moon reflected sunlight. The most advanced scientific work took place in Hellenistic times (pp. 62–63). An important area of Greek science was medicine. The Greeks believed that illness was a punishment sent by the gods to whom they prayed for a cure. Sanctuaries of the god Asclepius (the god of medicine) were found all over the Greek world. The most famous one was at Epidaurus. Many sick people came there and spent the night in the temple. They believed that Asclepius appeared to them in "dreams" to prescribe treatments such as herbal remedies, diets, and exercises. The next day, the priests would carry out the treatment and many people went away cured. The Greeks developed sophisticated medical treatments for all kinds of diseases. These treatments, based on practical research, grew out of the Asclepiad cult and were practiced by Hippocrates (460–377 BCE), who is often described as the founder of modern medicine.

Antikythera mechanism

The inner workings of the mechanism were originally fronted by a brass plate with a dial that showed the positions of astronomical bodies

The different parts of the mechanism are all very corroded, and some are stuck together

THE ANTIKYTHERA MECHANISM
This device was found in the wreck of a ship that sank in 82 BCE off the Greek island of Antikythera. Made of bronze and about 13 in (33 cm) high, the shoebox-sized device would originally have been mounted in a wooden frame. The complexity of the clocklike mechanism, which contained more than 30 gears, stunned experts. X-ray analysis of the heavily corroded parts revealed that the Antikythera mechanism was probably an early type of "computer." When dates were entered via a crank, the mechanism indicated the relative positions of the Sun, Moon, and planets. It was most likely used for navigation, or perhaps for astrological or astronomical calculations.

IT ALL ADDS UP
This engraving from the *Margarita Philosophica* of 1496 shows the Roman philosopher Boethius (480–524 CE) doing mathematical calculations, and the Greek mathematician Pythagoras (pp. 46–47) working at an abacus. The woman in the center is probably a muse of learning.

TEMPLE OF ASCLEPIUS
In this engraving, people can be seen approaching a statue of the god Asclepius. He is sitting on a throne and holding his staff which has a serpent twisted around it. A real snake, regarded as sacred and kept in all temples to Asclepius, can be seen slithering along the plinth.

TEMPLE VISIT
In this painting by the 19th-century artist John William Waterhouse (1849–1917) a child has been brought by his mother to the temple of Asclepius. Priests of the god stand around waiting to interpret his wishes.

THANKS

Patients who had been cured by Asclepius often left a model of the part of their body affected by illness, as an offering of thanks to the god for curing them. This marble relief of a leg has an inscription to Asclepius carved upon it and was dedicated by a worshiper named Tyche.

ΑϹΚΛΗ
ΠΙΩ
ΚΑΙ
ΫΓΕΙΑ
ΤΥΧΗ
ΕΥΧΑΡΙϹ
ΤΗΡΙΟΝ

HIPPOCRATES

The famous physician, Hippocrates, was born on the island of Kos. He wrote 53 scientific books on medical topics, now known as the *Corpus*. He taught that the human body was a single organism and each part could only be understood in the context of the whole. Modern doctors still take the Hippocratic Oath which is the basis of medical ethics.

MODERN MODELS

The practice of leaving a model of the affected part of the body as a thanks offering still continues in churches in some countries today. These modern examples are from Athens.

TOKENS

These modern silver tokens are also thanks for cures. The animals indicate that people believed that they too could be cured with the help of offerings.

Death and the afterlife

THE DIVER
This delightful painting was found on the inside of a stone sarcophagus (coffin) found at Poseidonia, a Greek city in southern Italy, later called Paestum. It probably represents the leap of the dead into the unknown.

KING OF THE UNDERWORLD
Zeus ruled the earth and sky, Poseidon, the sea. The third of these divine brothers was Hades, king of the underworld, also known as Pluto. Eventually the underworld came to be known simply as Hades.

DEATH CAME EARLY for most people in ancient times, because life was very harsh. Young men often died in battle and young women in childbirth. The Greeks believed in—or hoped for— some kind of life after death, although their ideas about this state varied. The kingdom of the dead was generally thought to be deep in the earth, and therefore many people buried their dead. But sometimes corpses were cremated on a funeral pyre. The soul was sometimes shown as a tiny winged person, and some Greeks believed that it escaped from the body and rose up to become one of the stars, waiting until it could be reborn in a new body. Gods, such as Dionysus, who, like the vines he protected, died and was reborn each year, gave people hope of new life. The goddess of the grain, Demeter, whose daughter Persephone was snatched away by Hades, the god of the underworld, claimed back her daughter for part of the year (spring and summer), too. Tombs were decorated with pictures of feasts and the dead person's favorite things, and food was placed in the grave so that the dead could be happy in the afterlife.

FLASK OF FAREWELL
Offerings to the dead included narrow flasks known as *lekythoi*, which contained oil used to anoint the body. They were decorated with delicately painted scenes of farewell. This dead warrior, perhaps a victim of one of the many wars in fifth-century Greece, receives his helmet from a woman. The goose at their feet, the bird of Aphrodite (pp. 20–21) hints at their relationship.

FARE FOR THE FERRYMAN

Charon was the grim ferryman who carried people across the black waters of the River Styx and into the kingdom of the dead. In this painting by John Stanhope (pp. 12–13), the underworld is a gloomy place with whispering reeds and spindly trees through which dead souls can be seen making their way to the river. The one-way trip in Charon's punt cost one obol. The family of the dead sometimes left a coin on the corpse for the journey.

THE ENTRANCE TO HADES

Ancient people thought that certain places might be the entrance to the underworld. Many Greeks had settled near Solfatara in southern Italy, where the steaming sulfur lake made it a prime candidate.

DEATH BEFORE DISHONOR

After the death of Achilles, the great warrior Ajax failed to become the champion of the Greeks fighting at Troy. He could not live with the shame, so killed himself by falling on his sword. This famous incident from the Trojan War is often shown on painted pots and is also the subject of a play by Sophokles (pp. 38–39).

TOMBSTONE

In Athens at certain periods, tombstones, carved in marble and originally painted in bright colors, were placed above graves. Above the carving of the dead person, the sloping lines of a roof suggested a temple or shrine. Here the dead man, Xanthippos, sits on an elegant curved chair, his children shown on a smaller scale beside him. His name is carved above him. It is not really known why he was holding a foot; possibly he was a shoemaker.

MOURNING LINE

A Greek funeral was a dramatic event. The body was laid out on a couch, with the feet facing the door to ensure that the spirit would leave. A wreath was placed on the head. A procession of mourners wearing black robes escorted the corpse. The women cut off their long hair as a sign of grief and gave a lock of it to the dead person. They also tore at their cheeks until the blood ran.

Alexander and the Hellenistic age

IN THE FOURTH CENTURY BCE, a strong king called Philip II turned Macedonia, in the north, into the most powerful state in Greece. After his assassination in 337 BCE, his 20-year-old son Alexander, a military genius, took over the reins of power. Not content with ruling Greece, he invaded Persian territory in 334 BCE, and then pressed on through Asia Minor, then south and east to Egypt, Afghanistan, and India. He established new Greek cities, such as Alexandria in Egypt, and thus spread Greek culture over a vast area. Alexander, called the Great, intended to create a huge empire, incorporating most of the then known world. His death of a fever in 323 BCE ended this ambition, and instead, his vast empire was divided up among his quarreling generals. The period from the death of Alexander until about 30 BCE is known as the Hellenistic Age from the word "Hellene," meaning Greek. The Hellenistic kingdoms preserved many aspects of Greek life but they were eventually overcome by the rising power of Rome.

EXCAVATION AT EPHESUS
Ephesus was a teeming city on the coast of Asia Minor where Greeks and people of many other nationalities lived together. The city and its famous sanctuary, dedicated to the goddess Artemis, thrived in the Hellenistic period and throughout the Roman period.

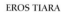

ONE MAN AND HIS DOG
This charming ring from the Hellenistic period is decorated with a scene of a shepherd with his dog and his crook.

APHRODITE
Terra-cotta figurines of Aphrodite, goddess of love and beauty, were popular in Hellenistic times. She is nearly always shown without any clothes, sometimes tying a ribbon in her hair, sometimes bending down to fasten her sandal.

Ruins at Pergamum

Ruins at Pergamum

TOWN PLANNING
Pergamum, a Hellenistic city in Asia Minor, was the power base of the wealthy Attalid dynasty. The ruins of temples and other opulent civic buildings can still be seen on the terraces cut into the steep mountain site. The people of Pergamum must have enjoyed spectacular views over the surrounding countryside.

EROS TIARA
Alexander's troops captured a great deal of Persian gold, and gold jewelry became very fashionable in aristocratic circles. Elaborate diadems, closely resembling crowns, have been found. Fixed at the front of this spectacular one is a tiny figure of Eros, the personification of love, holding a jug.

ALEXANDER'S EMPIRE

Alexander did not just want to build an empire, he also wanted it to last. To stop rebellion and invasion by conquered peoples, he founded many colonies populated by his own former soldiers who followed the Greek way of life. On the whole he treated the conquered peoples with respect and encouraged his men to marry Eastern women. His conquests came to an end in India because his men refused to fight any further.

Richard Burton in the 1956 film
Alexander the Great

TRUNK CHARGER

This coin shows Alexander on horseback attacking two Indian warriors mounted on an elephant. It is thought to have been issued in Babylon in 323 BCE.

WALL OF FIRE

Alexander entered India in 327 BCE and defeated Poros, a local ruler. When his troops refused to march farther east, he turned south down the Indus river to the sea. Alexander's fame lived on in legend. This Indian painting shows him building a defensive wall of fire.

THE DEFEAT OF DARIUS

Alexander finally defeated the Persian king Darius III in a long and bloody battle at Gaugamela in Mesopotamia (south-west Asia) in 331 BCE, and Darius fled. After this, Alexander called himself "King of Asia." In this etching, he can be seen on horseback, fighting fearlessly.

FAMILY OF DARIUS

In this painting by the Italian artist Paolo Veronese (1528–1588), Alexander is shown receiving the submission of the family of his defeated enemy Darius. Notice that the artist has dressed everyone in 16th-century clothes.

Did you know?

FASCINATING FACTS

Pan, Greek god of fields, shepherds, and woodlands, was believed to have a terrifying voice, which could paralyze animals with fear, stop armies from advancing, and topple city walls. The god's name is the root of our word *panic*.

The apparently upright, tapering columns on the Parthenon actually lean inward slightly and bulge in the middle. This is to compensate for the effects of perspective, which visually distorts straight lines and accurate alignments. For the same reason, the Parthenon frieze is sculpted in deeper relief toward the top, and the building's base and steps are imperceptibly higher in the middle than at the edges.

No mortar was used in the construction of Greek temples: stone blocks were smoothly fitted together and held with metal clamps and dowels.

The ancient Greeks established a tradition of making and decorating pottery that lasted for over 1,000 years. Some of the objects they produced look very strange to us—cups and bottles, for example, that could not be set down on a flat surface because they had curved or pointed bases. Many others, though, such as simple rounded jugs and storage pots, are almost exactly the same as the ones in a twenty-first century kitchen.

Color was very important to the ancient Greeks, especially in the Hellenistic period (from 323 to about 30 BCE). In fact, many of the white marble statues we associate with this time were once brightly painted.

Alexander the Great was given his horse Bucephalus, when he was 12 years old. No adult could control the animal, but Alexander discovered that the horse was frightened of his own shadow, so he calmed him by turning his head to the sun.

Greek god Pan playing a lyre

Macedonian soldiers originated a battle line called a phalanx, in which they would huddle close together forming a compact mass with their shields. This powerful unit would then push and shove its way through enemy lines.

The Greeks invented picture mosaics in the fifth century BCE. They used the new technique to decorate their floors with elaborate mythological scenes. The first mosaics were made from colored pebbles, but these were later replaced with specially cut cubes of glass, stone, or marble called *tesserae*, which produced finer detail and a larger range of colors.

Alexander and his horse

Lion Gate, Mycenae, erected in the thirteenth century BCE

The prehistoric Mycenaeans built such huge stone walls around their citadels—some of them were 46 ft (14 m) wide—that later civilizations believed they were the work of giants.

The distinctive proportions and one-foot-forward stance typical of kouroi (male nude temple statues) were adopted from ancient Egyptian figures. Monumental in size, they were idealized rather than naturalistic in style.

Slaves were very important to the economy of ancient Greece. Some had very hard lives, but many were respectfully treated and well educated. Those taken prisoner by the Romans after their conquest were highly prized, and some worked as teachers and doctors.

Greek theaters, with their tiered seating, were very sophisticated in terms of sight lines and sound amplification. They had to be built into natural slopes, though, since the Greeks did not have the engineering skills to support the necessary height and weight of the buildings on flat ground.

Archimedes, legendary mathematician and scientist, was murdered by the Romans in 212 BCE during their conquest of Greek territories. This conquest was complete by 146 BCE.

QUESTIONS AND ANSWERS

Q What happened when the ancient Greeks consulted the Oracle of Apollo at Delphi?

A Those who wanted advice from the Oracle would be required to sacrifice an animal on the altar. The petitioner was then led into the presence of the priestess and would ask a question. Although she was in a trance, the priestess answered questions clearly. Some replies were later turned into verses, and from these the Delphi Oracle gained a reputation for giving confusing responses.

Q Why was Delphi considered a sacred place?

A According to legend, the god Zeus released two eagles from opposite ends of the Earth. Their paths crossed above Delphi, which established it as the center of the world, and a sacred site. The spot was originally marked out with a navel stone or omphalos, a Hellenistic copy of which can be seen in the Delphi Museum. The young god Apollo was thought to live at Delphi, which is why, from the end of the eighth century BCE, people came here to ask his advice.

Temple of Apollo at Delphi

Q Where did traditional Greek drama come from?

A Greek drama developed in the sixth century BCE from ritual role-playing during festivals of Dionysus, the god of revelry and wine. At first, the participants danced in groups and were often dressed as animals. Later, singing and dancing choruses were joined by actors wearing masks with exaggerated features to indicate the characters they were playing so they could be clearly seen by everyone in the audience. The first proper plays were tragedies in the form of episodes from myths and epic poems. They were staged in sets of three, all written by the same person. Comedy did not appear on the Greek stage until about 480 BCE.

Q Where did the tradition of the marathon run come from?

A In 490 BCE, the Greeks were facing invasion by Darius of Persia, whose warships landed in the Bay of Marathon. Despite being heavily outnumbered, the Greeks surrounded the enemy troops and drove them back to the sea, losing only 192 men during the fighting, while 6,000 Persians perished. News of the victory was taken back to Athens—a distance of 26 miles (41 km)—by a runner in full armor, who collapsed and died immediately afterwards. The modern marathon has its roots in this heroic effort.

Q Why is classical Greek architecture so widely admired?

A State and religious buildings in ancient Greece were designed and built with the express intention of embodying perfect form and proportion. The degree of success their architects achieved is illustrated by the fact that their classical style has survived, has seldom fallen out of fashion, and has often dominated aesthetic taste. Superb examples were built in revolutionary France, Georgian England, the newly formed United States, and nineteenth-century Athens, where Neoclassical architecture completely dominated public building (see pages 68–69).

Record Breakers

FIRST OF THE GREATS
The Greek warrior king Alexander (356–323 BCE) was the first leader to be widely known as "the Great." During his short life, he founded 70 cities, several of which were named Alexandria after him.

EARLY LEARNING
Aristotle, a pupil of Plato, founded the Lyceum in Athens where subjects as diverse as biology and ethics could be taught. This institution turned Athens into one of the first university cities in the world.

FIRST STONE THEATER
The first stone theater ever built, and the birthplace of Greek tragedy, was the Theater of Dionysus, which was cut into the southern cliff face of the Acropolis. The remains of a restored and redesigned Roman version can still be seen there today.

EARLY RECORDS
Greek historians dated events by the Olympic Games. They calculated that the first games took place in 776 BCE. Named for the Sanctuary of Olympia on the Peloponnese peninsula, where they were held, the games originally had only one event—men's sprinting—and the runners were all local. Later, other competitions, such as wrestling, boxing, jumping, javelin throwing, and riding, were added, and the games were open to people from other parts of Greece.

Decoration from prizewinner's pot from the Panathenaic Games in Athens

Men competed naked in the games; women did not compete at all

Who's who?

NO OTHER SINGLE CULTURE has influenced Western civilization more profoundly than that of ancient Greece. Over a period of a few hundred years, this warm land between the Mediterranean, Aegean, and Ionian seas produced an unequaled collection of statesmen, writers, and artists, men of science, and great thinkers whose ideas and innovations are still widely valued.

STATESMEN

SOLON
Athenian legislator and magistrate during the seventh and sixth centuries BCE, whose legal, economic, and political reforms represented the birth of democracy.

THEMISTOCLES
Leader of Athens and creator of the powerful fleet that overpowered the Persians at the battle of Salamis in 480 B.CE.

PERICLES
Powerful general and great democratic leader of Athens in the fifth century B.CE. Cultured and incorruptible, Pericles masterminded an extensive public building program that included the Acropolis.

Statue of Pericles

ALEXANDER THE GREAT
Born to Philip II of Macedonia in 356 BCE and taught by Aristotle, Alexander expanded the Greek Empire into Persia, Asia Minor, Egypt, Afghanistan, and India before he died at age 33.

Eighteenth-century relief portrait of Alexander the Great

WRITERS AND ARTISTS

PHEIDIAS
The most famous artist of the ancient world (he died around 432 BCE), he was celebrated in his own time for two giant statues, one of Athena and one of Zeus. Neither statue still exists, and today he is best known for the Parthenon carvings, which he designed and supervised.

AESCHYLUS
One of three playwrights (with Euripides and Sophocles) dominating Athenian drama in the fifth century BCE. A soldier who fought at Marathon, Aeschylus produced nearly 90 plays, including *Prometheus Bound* and the *Oresteia*.

EURIPIDES
Athenian playwright (see above) who created controversial tragedies in the fifth century BCE, with themes of betrayal, murder, and injustice. Surviving examples of his plays include *Medea* and *Alcestis*.

SOPHOCLES
Athenian poet and playwright of the fifth century BCE (see above), known for powerful works such as *Ajax* and *Antigone*.

SAPPHO
Lyric poetess who led a group of female writers on the Aegean island of Lesbos in the seventh century BCE Sappho wrote mainly about family and female friends.

MYRON
Athenian sculptor of the fifth century BCE. With much of his work lost, Myron is best known today for his bronze statue *The Discus Thrower*, which survives only as Roman copies.

The Discus Thrower (also known as Discobulus)

This Roman copy is made of marble

THINKERS

PYTHAGORAS
Philosopher and mathematician of the sixth century BCE who believed that the secrets of life lay in mathematics.

HERODOTUS
Fifth-century BCE historian, known as the father of history, who produced the first prose accounts of current events, such as the Greek war with the Persians.

THUCYDIDES
Another historian of the fifth century BCE, Thucydides documented the Peloponnesian war between Athens and Sparta using a very analytical approach.

SOCRATES
Renowned fifth-century BCE thinker who produced no written work, but instead explored ideas through discussion. His talks, as documented by his pupil, Plato, are known as "dialogues."

PLATO
Pupil of Socrates who recorded his teacher's work and set up an Academy in Athens. Plato, too, believed in dialogues, and he produced two well-known treatises, *The Republic* and *The Laws*. Plato was also one of the greatest Greek prose writers.

ARISTOTLE
Fourth-century BCE pupil of Plato and founder of the Lyceum, Aristotle had an outstanding gift for scientific observation, and one of his most valued legacies is a treatise on Ethics.

EPICURUS
Greek philosopher during the fourth and third centuries BCE. He taught that genuine human happiness is the highest good, and he encouraged its responsible pursuit. Author of a 37-book treatise called *On Nature*, he founded the Epicurean school of philosophy.

Socrates

SCIENTISTS

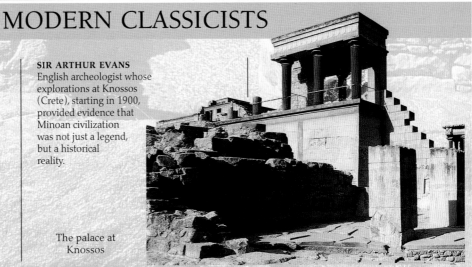
Hippocrates

ANAXAGORAS
Astronomer of the fifth century BCE who discovered that the Moon reflects light from the Sun.

HIPPOCRATES
Founder of modern medicine in the fifth and fourth centuries BCE, Hippocrates practiced it according to the strict ethical standard which doctors still adhere to today in the Hippocratic Oath. He also discovered the painkilling effects of willow bark, from which modern scientists extracted aspirin.

ARISTARCHUS
Third-century BCE astronomer who understood that the Earth revolves around the Sun and that it rotates on its own axis.

ASCLEPIADES
Physician of the first century BCE who was learned in medicine and compassionate in his treatment of patients. Like some modern practitioners, he advocated holistic, noninvasive treatments. His treatments included such things as wine, massage, and bathing.

MODERN CLASSICISTS

SIR WILLIAM HAMILTON
Early nineteenth-century British diplomat and expert on Greek art. His collection of vases was acquired by the British Museum.

HEINRICH SCHLIEMANN
German amateur archeologist who, in 1870, discovered the site of ancient Troy near the Turkish coast. This discovery supplied a factual basis for Homer's epic tales of the Trojan war.

PIERRE DE COUBERTIN
Aristocratic Frenchman who, inspired by the original Olympic games, organized the first modern revival in Athens in 1896.

SIR ARTHUR EVANS
English archeologist whose explorations at Knossos (Crete), starting in 1900, provided evidence that Minoan civilization was not just a legend, but a historical reality.

The palace at Knossos

Find out more

THE INFLUENCE OF ANCIENT GREECE has spread throughout almost every country in the Western world, and most major museums have a section devoted to Greek art and antiquities. Perhaps the culture's best-known and most powerful symbol, however, is the fortified citadel complex of the Acropolis in Athens with its sacred center, the Parthenon.

Created as a temple to Athena, patron goddess of Athens, the Parthenon was completely symmetrical. It was constructed of stone and locally quarried white marble, an ideal medium for the detailed relief panels on the frieze and portico. During its long history, the Parthenon has been a church, a mosque, and even an arsenal, but today, its inspiring ruins are a popular tourist attraction and a place of pilgrimage for anyone with a fascination for the classical world.

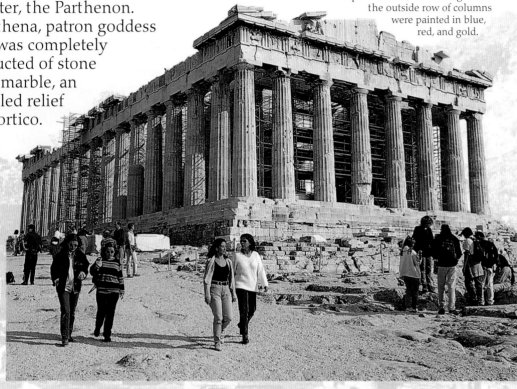

THE PARTHENON
Completed in the mid-fifth century BCE, the Parthenon was designed by the architects Kallikrates and Iktinos to house a monumental 40 ft (12 m) statue of Athena sculpted by Pheidias. When the temple was new, the carvings above the outside row of columns were painted in blue, red, and gold.

Skillful carving gives an impression of great depth

THE PARTHENON FRIEZE
The carved frieze that ran around the inner wall of the Parthenon was designed by Pheidias, the artist responsible for all the carving and sculpture in the temple. The individual segments of the frieze are called *metopes*; together they portray a procession of worshipers taking part in the Panathenaic festival, which was held every four years to celebrate Athena's birthday. This section is on display at the British Museum in London.

Mask is made of gold

MASK OF AGAMEMNON
Discovered at Mycenae by Heinrich Schliemann (see page 67), this death mask in the National Archeological Museum of Athens dates from about 1500 BCE. Experts now know that it does not portray the legendary king, Agamemnon, who led the Greek forces in the Trojan war, but the object's longstanding fame makes it difficult to alter the name by which it is best known.

Places to visit

METROPOLITAN MUSEUM OF ART, NEW YORK, NEW YORK
With a dedicated area that extends over both its main floors, the Metropolitan Museum's Greek and Roman galleries feature:
- a large collection of ancient Greek vases
- important examples of painting and sculpture that illustrate the classical mastery of naturalism in art.

THE ACROPOLIS, ATHENS, GREECE
Although access to the temples is restricted to protect them from further damage, the Acropolis still offers a unique collection of ancient sites and exhibits, including:
- the Parthenon
- the Propylaia and the Beule Gate, historical entrances to the complex
- the Theater of Dionysus, birthplace of Greek tragedy, built in 342–326 BCE.
- the Acropolis Museum, which displays a wealth of treasures from the site, including statues and architectural details such as caryatids, pediments, and segments of the Parthenon frieze.

ANCIENT DELPHI, GREECE
First excavated at the end of the nineteenth century, this site encompasses:
- the Sanctuary of Apollo
- the Castalian Spring, where visitors were required to bathe
- the stadium where the panhellenic Pythian Games took place

NATIONAL ARCHEOLOGICAL MUSEUM, ATHENS, GREECE
Housed in a nineteenth-century building that has been constantly expanded and improved, this is one of the world's most important collections. Among its treasures are:
- the gold mask of Agamemnon, around 1500 BCE, which was found at Mycenae
- superb examples of classical sculpture, including the Marathon Boy dating from around 340 BCE

BRITISH MUSEUM, LONDON, ENGLAND
One of the finest collection of Greek antiquities in the world is on display here. Look for:
- the Parthenon marbles (also known as the Elgin marbles)—sculptures and sections of the frieze brought to England by Lord Elgin in the early nineteenth century
- a huge statue from the Mausoleum at Halicarnassus, one of the Seven Wonders of the Ancient World

GETTY VILLAGE, MALIBU, CALIFORNIA
This branch of the Getty Museum features a wealth of ancient Greek and Roman art, at a site whose architecture and setting reflects the beauty of the classical Mediterranean world. Visitors to the Villa can enjoy:
- more than 1,200 objects from the classical world, including sculptures of mythological heroes
- an annual outdoor theater production, often an ancient Greek play

Harvesters hit the branches with sticks to knock the olives to the ground

GREEK THEATER
This drawing of the character Creon from Sophokles' play *Antigone* comes from an 1899 issue of the French magazine *La Theatre*. The study of Greek theatrical tradition is one way we have been able to learn about classical Greek culture.

PAINTED JAR
Two-handled vessels with narrowed necks are called *amphoras*, and they were designed to store liquid (oil, wine, or water) or foods preserved in liquid. The detailed scene of olive-gathering painted on this example from the British Museum suggests that it was intended for olives or olive oil.

NATIONAL ARCHEOLOGICAL MUSEUM, ATHENS
Opened in 1891, this museum displays an enormous number of Greek works of art that had previously been stored all over the city. Designed in the Neoclassical style that harkens back to Greece's golden age, the building's entrance is dominated by Ionic and Corinthian columns.

MARATHON BOY
Found on the seafloor, like many other Greek bronzes, this graceful nude (in the National Archeological Museum, Athens), is thought to be the work of the sculptor Praxiteles, who was active in the fourth century BCE.

Glossary

ABACUS Ancient counting frame made up of small beads threaded on wires.

ACANTHUS Plant with thick scalloped leaves which often adorn Greek art and architecture. The capital on a Corinthian column is covered with acanthus leaves. (*see also* CAPITAL, CORINTHIAN)

Acanthus capital

AGORA Open market or public space in ancient Greece. Our modern term *agoraphobia*, meaning fear of public places, comes from this word.

AMPHORA Two-handled jar with a narrow neck and sometimes a tapered base, designed for wine, olive oil, or other liquid.

ANDRON Small, domestic dining room where men would entertain their friends.

ARYBALLOS Perfume pot, usually made of pottery. These vessels were often in the shape of a fantasy creature or a real animal, such as a monkey or a hedgehog.

Colonnade

ASSEMBLY Gathering of people and officials which controlled public life in ancient Athens. There had to be at least 6,000 present to make an Assembly, which decided on important matters of law and state. (*see also* COUNCIL)

ATLANTES Carved male figure used as a column in classical architecture. (*see also* CARYATID, COLUMN)

CAPITAL The top section of an architectural column, (*see also* COLUMN, CORINTHIAN, DORIC, IONIC, ORDER)

CARYATID Carved female figure used as a supporting column in classical architecture. (*see also* ATLANTES, COLUMN).

CHITON Basic item of clothing for both men and women in ancient Greece. *Chitons* were made from two rectangles of fabric fastened at the shoulders and down the sides, and tied at the waist. (*see also* PEPLOS)

CITY-STATE A conventional city, which, with its surrounding territory, is also an independent political state.

COLONNADE Line of columns supporting a row of arches, a roof, an upper story or the top part of a wall.

COLUMN A slender, upright structure used in architecture to support an arch, a roof, an upper story, or the top part of a wall. Most columns consist of a base, shaft (the main part), and capital (the decorative section at the top). (*see also* CAPITAL, ORDER)

CORINTHIAN One of three principal styles (or orders) in classical architecture. Corinthian columns fall between those of the Doric and Ionic orders in diameter and width of fluting, and they have elaborate, bell-shaped capitals adorned with acanthus leaves. (*see also* ACANTHUS, DORIC, IONIC, ORDER)

COUNCIL Five-hundred strong advisory body which arranged the business of the Athenian Assembly. (*see also* ASSEMBLY)

CUIRASS Body armor, usually made of bronze, worn by Greek soldiers to protect their back and chest.

DEMOCRACY A system of government in which the people being governed have a voice, usually through elected representatives.

DORIC One of three principal styles (or orders) in classical architecture. Doric columns are solid with wide fluting and a plain, round capital. (*see also* CORINTHIAN, IONIC, ORDER)

ELECTRUM Alloy of gold and silver that was used to make early Greek coins. Later coins were made of pure silver or sometimes gold.

EPINETRON Semicylindrical instrument used by Greek women to prepare wool for spinning. Often highly decorated, epinetrons fit over one knee.

In fresco painting, pigments are absorbed into wet plaster to fix their colors.

Fourteenth-century fresco prepared in a similar way to those of ancient Greece

FRESCO Wall painting applied to plaster when it is wet. Frescoes were popular in many warm countries until the Middle Ages. (*see also* MURAL)

FRIEZE A deep band of decoration running along the upper part of a wall.

GALLEY Ancient Greek or Roman warship powered by one or more rows of oars.

GRAMMATISTES Teacher of core subjects such as reading, writing, and mathematics. (*see also* KITHARISTES, PAIDOTRIBES)

GREAVES Bronze leg guards worn by Greek soldiers for protection in battle.

GRIFFIN Mythical creature with the head and wings of an eagle and the body of a lion.

Griffin

GYMNASIUM Large room or building used for physical exercise and training.

GYNAECEUM Women's quarters in a Greek home, where looms for weaving, and children's toys and furniture would be found.

HETAIRAI Group of witty, beautiful women whose main function was to play music, dance, and entertain men at dinner parties.

HIMATION Outer cloak worn by ancient Greeks. This garment was traditionally pulled under the right arm and draped over the left shoulder.

HIPPOCAMP Mythical seahorse with two front feet and the tail of a fish or dolphin.

HOPLITE Fully armed Greek foot soldier, from *hoplon*, meaning shield.

IONIC One of three principal styles (or orders) in classical architecture. Ionic columns are slender with narrow fluting and a scrolled capital. (*see also* DORIC, CORINTHIAN, ORDER, VOLUTE)

KTTHARISTES Teacher of music. A *kithara* is an instrument much like a lyre, only larger. (*see also* GRAMMATISTES, PAIDOTRIBES)

KOUROS Marble statue of a naked boy, usually used as a cult statue.

KYLIX Shallow, footed drinking cup with two handles.

LABYRINTH Intricate and confusing network of passages formed by walls or hedges.

LYRE Stringed Greek instrument with a hollow body that was originally made from a tortoise shell.

MURAL Wall painting on dry plaster. (*see also* FRESCO)

OINOCHOE A wine jug with a long neck, made either of pottery or metal, and often decorated.

ORACLE Sacred place where ancient Greeks could ask their gods, through a priestess, to give them advice or to foretell the future. The most famous oracle was that of Apollo at Delphi.

ORCHESTRA Flat circular area where the actors and chorus performed in a Greek theater.

ORDER One of several styles of classical architecture defined by shape and proportion. The three best-known orders are Doric, Ionic, and Corinthian (see page 27). (*see also* CORINTHIAN, DORIC, IONIC)

OSTRAKON Fragment of stone of pottery

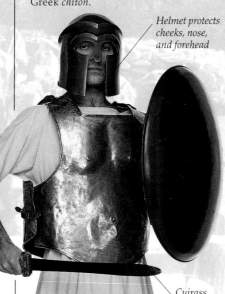

Early lyre with tortoiseshell body inscribed with writing or drawing.

PAIDOGOGOS Domestic slave with particular responsibility for accompanying Greek boys to school.

PAIDOTRIBES Teacher of physical exercise such as athletics or wrestling. (*see also* KITHARISTES, GRAMMATISTES)

PALAISTRA Specially designed building, smaller than a gymnasium, with dressing rooms and a sand-covered courtyard where Greek boys were taught athletics and wrestling.

PEDIMENT Triangular gable end on a building; decorative, triangular architectural motif positioned above a door.

PEPLOS An early, simpler, version of the Greek *chiton*.

Helmet protects cheeks, nose, and forehead

Cuirass

Greaves

Hoplite

PYXIS Small container or casket in which Greek women kept cosmetics.

SLAVE Man, woman, or child who is owned by another person like an item of property, usually to do work of some kind.

STOA Long, colonnaded structure with a wall on one side, where people traditionally met to talk and conduct business.

STRATEGOS One of ten elected military leaders responsible for making decisions about the defense of ancient Athens or concerning its involvement in a war.

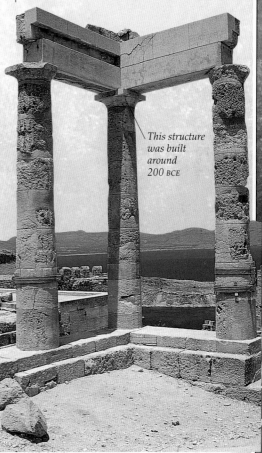

This structure was built around 200 BCE

Ruined *stoa* on the island of Lindos

SYMPOSIA All-male drinking parties. Small, private *symposia* were held in private homes; when numbers increased, public buildings would be used.

THOLOS Round, domed building in which the members of the government Council met. (*see also* COUNCIL)

TRIREME Fast warship powered by up to 170 oarsmen positioned over three levels on either side of the hull.

TYRANT Absolute ruler of a Greek city-state who had usually seized power by force.

VOLUTE Spiral-like scroll used on Ionic capitals and sometimes on pottery vessels. (*see also* CAPITAL, COLUMN, IONIC)

Index

A

Achilles, 12, 13, 35, 55, 61
Acropolis, 7, 16, 17, 18, 25, 27, 38, 65, 66, 68, 69
Aegean Sea, 6, 8, 23, 31
Aegina, 40, 52
Aeschylus, 66
Agamemnon, King, 10, 11, 12, 39, 68
agora, 16, 25, 32, 52, 70
Ajax, 35, 61
Alexander the Great, 7, 27, 46, 62–63, 64, 65, 66
Alexandria, 62, 63, 65
Alma-Tadema, Sir Lawrence, 30, 42
Alpheios River, 26
amphora, 48, 49, 70
Anaxagoras, 67
Aphrodite, 20, 31, 41, 60, 62
Apollo, 6, 19, 20, 21, 24, 25, 27, 32, 65
Archer, A., 17
Archimedes, 64
architecture, 64, 65, 68
Aristophanes, 58, 67
Aristotle, 46, 47, 65, 67
armor, 10, 54–55
Artemis, 20, 21, 27, 32, 52, 57, 62
aryballos, 7, 14, 15, 49, 70
Asclepiades, 58, 59, 67
Asia, 54, 63
Asia Minor, 6, 27, 35, 52, 62
astronomy, 67
Athena, 7, 16–17, 21, 23, 25, 27, 44, 45, 57, 68
Athens, 6, 7, 16–19, 21, 30, 59, 61, 62, 65, 69
Academy, 47, 67
Acropolis, 27, 68, 69
Panathenaea, 7, 16, 25, 44, 68
Pireaus, 16, 56
pottery, 48
soldiers, 54
theater, 38
athletes, 7, 26, 33, 40, 41, 44, 45, 65

B

Babylon, 58, 63
banquets, 31, 36, 50
Bellerophon, 23
Beule Gate, 69
Black Sea, 7, 14, 23

Boethius, 58
Britain, 7, 39
British Museum, 6, 17, 68, 69
Bronze Age, 7, 8, 10, 50
Bucephalus, 64
Burton, Richard, 63
Byron, Lord, 26

CD

Castalian Spring, 69
chariot, 25, 54
chiton, 40, 42, 43, 70
city-states, 6, 16, 18, 52, 54, 70
Classical Period, 7, 16, 42
cloak, 40, 42, 43
coins, 17, 19, 23, 52, 61, 63, 64
colonies, 15, 26, 27, 42, 63
color, importance, 64
columns, 64, 70
comedy, 65
Corinth, 6, 14, 27, 41, 49, 63
Corinthian order, 27, 70
Cosimo, Piero di, 22
Coubertin, Baron Pierre de, 45, 67
crafts, 7, 10, 14, 23, 52, 56
Crete, 6, 7, 8–9, 10, 50, 67
Cruikshank, George, 56
Cyprus, 10, 20, 52, 63
Daedalus, 23
Daphne, 21
Darius, King, 65
Dark Age, 7, 10, 12, 14
Degas, Edgar, 56
deities, 6, 21, 26, 52
Delphi, 6, 19, 21, 24, 25, 38, 44, 65, 69
Demeter, 20, 21, 24, 26, 50, 60
democracy, 7, 18, 66
Dionysus, 20, 25, 38, 46, 47, 48, 60, 65
Discobulus, 6
Doric order, 27, 70

EF

education, 30, 32–33, 65
Egypt, 7, 8, 14, 58, 62, 63, 64
Electra, 39
electrum, 52, 70
Eleusis, 6
Elgin, Lord, 17
Elgin marbles, 69
Ephesus, 6, 14, 27, 52, 62
Epicurus, 67
Epidauros, 38, 58
epinetron, 31, 70

Erechtheion, 27
Eros, 20, 22, 62
Euripides, 38, 66
Eurotas River, 56, 57
Evans, Sir Arthur, 9, 67
festivals, 24–25, 38, 41, 44, 48, 50
fishing, 50, 52, 53

GH

Gaia, 20
games, 7, 20, 24, 25, 32, 34, 35, 40, 44–45, 65
garments, 40, 42–43
grain, 8, 20, 21, 24, 28, 50
grammatistes, 33, 70
graves, 10, 11, 32, 33, 39, 40, 51, 60–61
gymnasium, 33, 71
gynaeceum, 28, 71
Hades, 60
Hamilton, Sir William, 42, 48, 67
Hektor, 12, 13, 55
Helen, 12, 14
Hellenistic Period, 7, 22, 42, 58, 62
Hephaistos, 20, 21, 22
Herakles, 22, 48, 52
Hermes, 28
Herodotus, 35, 56, 67
hetairai, 31, 36, 39, 71
himation, 40, 43, 71
hippocamp, 7
Hippocrates, 58, 59, 67
Homer, 7, 11, 12, 67

IJK

Iktinos, 68
The Iliad, 12
India, 7, 62, 63
Iona, 6, 7, 27, 42
Ionic order, 27, 70
Italy, 7, 14, 24, 26, 27, 34, 46, 48, 54, 60, 61, 63
Jason, 23
jewelry, 10, 11, 12, 40, 52, 62
Kallikrates, 68
Kerameikos, 48
kithara, 23, 34
kitharistes, 33
Knossos, 6, 7, 67
Kos, 42, 59
Kouros, 6, 64, 71
kylix, 49, 71

LM

Labyrinth, 9, 71
Lesbos, 31, 66

Lion gate, 11, 64
Lyceum, 65, 67
Lydia, 6, 35, 52
lyre, 6, 41, 71
Macedonia, 6, 7, 20, 46, 62, 64
Marathon, 19, 65
marathon (modern), 65
mask of Agamemnon, 68, 69
Mausoleum at Halicarnassus, 69
medicine, 58–59, 67
Mediterranean, 8, 12, 14, 49, 52
Medusa, 23
Menelaus, King, 12
Mesopotamia, 63
Messenia, 56
metopes, 68
Minoa, 7, 8, 9, 10, 40, 67
Minos, King, 8
Minotaur, 8, 9
mosaics, 64
Muses, 25, 34, 39, 58
museums, 68–69
music, 25, 33, 34, 38, 46, 56
Mycenae, 6, 7, 10, 11, 12, 22, 64, 68
Myron, 66
mythology, 8, 22, 39, 41

NO

Naples, 26, 42
Odysseus, 12, 13, 14, 21
The Odyssey, 12
Oedipus, King, 39
olive oil, 8, 40, 41, 44, 49, 51, 52, 60
Olympia, 6, 26, 33, 44, 65
Olympic games, 7, 44–45, 65, 67
Olympus, Mount, 20
omphalos, 25, 65
oracle, 24, 25, 65, 71
orchestra, 38, 71
Orpheus, 23
ostrakon, 19, 71

P

paidogogos, 33, 71
paidotribes, 33, 71
palaces, 7, 8, 9, 10, 11, 12, 50
Pan, 20, 22, 41, 64
Panathenaea, 7, 16, 25, 44, 68
papyrus scrolls, 30, 33, 48
Parnassus, Mount, 25
Parthenon, 7, 16, 17, 64, 68, 69
Parthenon frieze, 64, 68

patron deity, 6, 21, 26
Pegasus, 23
Peloponnese, 7, 22, 65
peplos, 16, 42, 71
Pergamum, 6, 62, 63
Perikles, 7, 16, 17, 18, 27, 66
Persephone, 20, 21, 60
Perseus, 23
Persians, 6, 7, 16, 18, 19, 52, 54, 62, 63
phalanx, 64
Pheidias, 66, 68
Philip II, King, 62, 66
philosophy, 6, 21, 36, 46–47, 58, 67
Picasso, Pablo, 9
Plataea, 6
Plato, 47, 67
Pluto, 60
poetry, 7, 12, 23, 26, 31, 33, 34, 56, 65, 66
politics, 6, 18–19, 26, 30, 36
Pollaiuolo, Antonio del, 21
Polykleitos, 41
Poseidonia (Paestum), 24, 26, 60
pottery, 7, 10, 11, 33, 46, 48–49, 52, 53, 64
Propylaia, 69
Psyche, 22
Pythagoras, 46, 58, 67
pyxis, 15, 40, 49, 71

QRS

Raphael, 47
religion, 7, 10, 19, 20–23, 24, 26, 37, 44, 46
Rhodes, 10, 14, 41, 51
Romans, 64
Royal National Theater, 39
sacrifice, 65
Salamis, 19, 54
Santorini, 50
Sappho, 66
Savery, Roelandt, 23
Schliemann, Heinrich, 11, 12, 67, 68
scientists, 67
sculptures, 17, 26, 38, 39, 40, 46, 64, 66, 68
Sicily, 14, 27
slaves, 18, 28, 30, 32, 33, 34, 36, 40, 42, 50, 52, 64, 71
Socrates, 47, 65, 67
soldiers, 6, 12, 27, 33, 40, 54–55, 56, 63, 64
Solon, 66
Sophokles, 39, 61, 66
Sparta, 6, 7, 12, 54, 56–57, 63

spinning, 30, 31, 33, 40, 42
stadium, 25, 44
Stanhope, John, 13, 61
statues, 6, 16, 25, 26, 28, 39, 40, 41, 44, 45, 47, 64, 66
Styx, River, 61
symposia, 31, 36, 37, 71
Syria, 8, 14

T

Tanagra, 40
temples, 7, 16, 17, 19, 20, 24, 25, 26–27, 44, 52, 58, 61, 62, 64, 65, 68
tesserae, 64
theater, 34, 38, 39, 64, 65, 66, 69
Thebes, 6, 14, 63
Themistokles, 66
Theseus, 9
Thessaly, 20, 23
Thucydides, 67
Tiepolo, Giovanni, 12
toys, 32, 33, 50
trade, 8, 10, 12, 14, 15, 45, 52, 56
tragedy, 65
trireme, 54, 55, 71
Trojan War, 11, 12–13, 14, 21, 39, 55, 61, 67
Troy, 6, 12, 13, 61, 67
tunic, 40, 42, 43
Turkey, 12, 20, 27, 52

UVW

Uranos, 20
Veronese, Paolo, 63
warfare, 18, 44, 54–55, 60
warriors, 14, 35, 55, 57, 60, 61
Waterhouse, John William, 58
wax tablets, 33
weapons, 10, 54, 55
weaving, 28, 30, 31, 33, 40, 53
wine, 7, 8, 13, 20, 22, 25, 32, 36, 38, 48, 49, 50, 51, 52, 58
worship, 8, 11, 16, 20–23, 25, 27, 50, 59
wrestling, 33, 44, 45, 65

XYZ

Xerxes, 54
Zeus, 8, 20, 21, 22, 23, 26, 44, 45, 50, 60, 65

Acknowledgments

Dorling Kindersley would like to thank: The Department of Greek and Roman Antiquities, the British Museum for providing ancient artifacts for photography; Patsy Vanags of the British Museum Education Service for assisting with the text; Bill Gordon for his model farmhouse on pp. 28–29; Alan Meek for the armor & weapons on pp. 54–55. Helena Spiteri, Andrew Chiakli, & Toby Williams for modelling the clothes & armor. Anit Burger for hairdressing & makeup; Jane Parker for the index.

For this edition, the publisher would also like to thank: Dr. Hugh Bowden for assisting with revisions; Claire Bowers, David Ekholm-JAlbum, Sunita Gahir, Joanne Little, Nigel Ritchie, Susan St. Louis, Carey Scott, & Bulent Yusuf for the clip art; David Ball, Neville Graham, Rose Horridge, Joanne Little, & Sue Nicholson for the wall chart; BCP, Laragh Kedwell, Marianne Petrou, and Owen Peyton Jones for checking the digitized files.

The publisher would like to thank the following for their kind permission to reproduce their images:

Picture credits a=above, b=bottom, c=center, f=far, l=left, m=middle, r=right, t=top.

AKG-images: 66cra; Erich Lessing 64tl
American School of Classical Studies, Athens: 32cla
Ancient Art & Architecture Collection: 12tr, 44tl, 56cl, 63cr; R. Sheridan 58cl
The Art Archive: ET Archive 62crb
Ashmolean Museum, Oxford: 9tl
Bildarchiv Preussischer Kulturbestitz (Antikenmuseum Berlin): 33tr
The Bridgeman Art Library: British Library 60tl; The Fine Art Society, London 13tl, 58br; House of Masks, Delos 20tl; Houses of Parliament, Westminster, London 18br; National Archeological

Museum, Athens 35cr, 50cl; National Gallery, London 56cb; Private Collection 30tl, 42br; Roy Miles Fine Paintings, Private Collection 61tl; Staatliche Antikensammlung und Glyptothek, München 46c; The Vatican Museums 47clb
Corbis / Zefa: 62c; Damm 25cl; Araldo de Luca 17tc, 26tl; K. Scholz 19tr; Starfoto 50tl
DK Images: British Museum 16tr, 16bl, 16br, 17c, 17bc, 17br, 18tr, 19cla, 19clb, 19br, 20bl, 40tl 47tr, 47br, 48bc, 48br, 65tr, 65br, 67tr, 67clb, 69cla; Lin White 64tc, 64tcr
Ekdotike Athenon: 52bl
Getty: Allsport / Gray Mortimore 45cl; Allsport / Vandystadt 45c; Hulton Archive 45b; Image Bank 51c; Time Life Pictures / Mansell 11tl, 12tl 62tl
Sonia Halliday: 8tl, 11tc, 11tr, 12bl, 20tr, 25tl, 25tr, 25c, 33c, 44cr
Michael Holford: 6tr, 7tr, 9bl, 16tl, 20br, 21c
The Kobal Collection: 63c
Mary Evans Picture Library: 18tl, 26cl, 31cl, 35cr, 38tr, 39tl, 44b, 46tr, 46br, 47c, 47bc, 54c, 56tl, 56c, 56bl, 58tl, 58c, 58cr, 59, 63cb, 64br, 64bt, 69tc
The National Gallery, London: 9cr, 12br, 21tr,

22tr, 23bl, 63b
Anne Pearson: 24br
Photo DAI, Athens: (neg. Mykonos 70) 12cb
Photostage: Donald Cooper 39tc
Robert Harding Picture Library: 38cl, 49br, 52bc, 53cla, 59bl; G. White 16cra
Royal Ontario Museum: 17tl
Scala: 11bc, 20cla, 26b, 35tl, 38b, 41b, 44cla; Delphi Museum 34bl; Heraklion Museum 8b; The Vatican Museums 36tl

Illustrations: John Woodcock & John Hutchinson. **Maps:** Sallie Alane Reason

Wall chart: Corbis: David Lees br; **DK Images:** British Library fclb (Pottery); British Museum, London, UK, c, cl; Dr John Coates crb (Boat)

Jacket: *Front:* Corbis, b; British Museum, t.
Back: All images British Museum.

All other images © Dorling Kindersley.
For further information see:
www.dkimages.com